They are waiting to take us into
              the severed garden
Do you know how pale & wanton thrillful
         comes death on a strange hour
         unannounced, unplanned for
like a scaring over-friendly guest you've
         brought to bed
Death makes angels of us all
         & gives us wings
where we had shoulders
         smooth as raven's
              claws

No more money, no more fancy dress
This other Kingdom seems by far the best
until its other jaw reveals incest
& loose obedience to a vegetable law

I will not go
Prefer a Feast of Friends
To the Giant family

James Douglas Morrison
from An American Prayer

W9-AGX-512

MORRISON

A Feast of Friends

Frank Lisciandro

WARNER BOOKS

A Time Warner Company

Copyright © 1991
by Frank J. Lisciandro
All rights reserved

Design
Don French & Associates,
Santa Barbara

Photography
Unless otherwise indicated,
photographs are copyrighted
© 1991 by Frank Lisciandro

Photo credits

Photos on pp. 6, 18, 21, 23, 24, 25, 26 © Joseph Sia; pp. 31, 37 © Fud Ford; pp. 70, 86 © Gregg Winter; p. 66 © Dale Smith; pp. 11, 80, 81 © Susan Cuscuna; p. 87 © Ron Allan; pp. 49, 54, 99, 154 © Henry Diltz; pp. 78, 79, 170 © George Shuba; pp. 50, 74 © Don Paulsen; pp. 62, 88, 89 © Chuck Boyd/Flower Children Ltd.; pp. 8, 120, 131 Michael Ochs Archives/Venice, CA; pp. 55, 60 © Jim Marshall; pp. 143 © Howard Hopkins; p 115 © Gareth Blyth; p. 167 all photography by Jeff Simon; pp. 173, 175 photography by Bruce MacCallum; pp. 14, 152, 153 from the private collection of Pamela Courson Morrison.

Cover design by Don French.
Cover photo © 1991 by Frank Lisciandro.
Cover photo hand colored by Dave Maestrejuan.

*This is dedicated
to the ones I love.*

Acknowledgements

It would be almost impossible to thank everyone who contributed to the creation of this book but, it would be unthinkable to omit anyone. My gratitude to all the people I interviewed, whether they appear in these pages or not; their participation and insights are greatly appreciated. Thank you Bruce Conner, Jean Meyer, Jack Hirschman, Ned Moraghan, Penny Courson, Steve Richmond, Michael Ford, Paul Ferrara, Arthur Korb, Georgia Ferrara Pulos, Guy Webster, Doug Cameron, Richard Tanguay. I am also obliged to Andrew Hawley who helped throughout the creation of this book; Alison Martino, a source for finding people and images; Kathy Lisciandro for her patience and good council; Colette Lisciandro for quick and sure aesthetic decisions; Columbus Courson & Pearl Marie Courson for their support and generosity; Deborah Schroeder for concept and editorial assistance; Jeff Brouws who printed most of the black and white photos; Cynthia Anderson for much needed proofreading; Mel Parker for valued editorial suggestions; Greg Shaw for a timely set of dates and places; Michael Beiley, Ph. D. who lead me to a deeper awareness of Jim's psychological character; Gareth Blyth, a friend of Jim; and Michael J. Siddons, George Sargent, George Feist, Randy Johnson, Richard Sargent, Carla Hewit, Kathy Johnson, Color Services, Lynne Richardson, Rod Sweetland, Scott Reid, Lucy Brown.

Warner Books, Inc.
666 Fifth Avenue,
New York, NY 10103

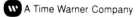 A Time Warner Company

Library of Congress Number:
91-50133

Printed in the United States
of America
First printing: April, 1991
10 9 8 7 6 5 4 3 2 1

Permissions
Permission to reproduce printed text from the following sources is gratefully acknowledged:
Villard Books: *Wilderness*, ©1988 by Columbus and Pearl Courson; *The American Night* ©1990 by Wilderness Publications.
Simon and Schuster: *The Lords and The New Creatures*, © 1969, 1970 by James Douglas Morrison.

SH 1325750

3P

Contents

THE QUESTION 9

VISIONS OF A CONCERT 13

AN ALLEGORY ~ *Vince Treanor (w/Bill Siddons)* 19

BEATNIKS ~ *Fud Ford (w/Larry Keenan)* 31

LITTLE BROTHER ~ *Philip O'Leno* 41

CONTROLLED CHAOS ~ *January Jansen* 55

UNPREDICTABLE ~ *Bill Siddons & Rich Linnell* 71

ON THE VERY EDGE ~ *Ron Allan* 87

RED LIGHTS ~ *Ginny Ganahl* 101

SNAKESKIN JACKET ~ *Michael McClure* 109

SHOOTING STAR ~ *Kathy Lisciandro & Cheri Siddons* 121

A COSMIC SPANKING ~ *Leon Barnard (w/Chris Boyle)* 133

THIS AFFAIR OF OURS ~ *Eva Gardoni Hormel* 145

NO FUTURE & NO PAST ~ *Babe Hill* 159

The Question

What we are searching for in all these clues and glimpses is a more accurate rendering, a more human and understandable portrait.

I n the past, when people discovered I was a friend of Jim Morrison, sooner or later they inevitably asked, "What was he really like?"; and I was able to supply an answer. But a simple, straightforward reply has become more difficult as sensational and conflicting fictions have obscured the truth about Jim.

Like other rock heroes whose lives ended too soon, Jim has become a cultural icon. Now the tabloids and magazines, Sunday supplements and MTV devote columns and air time to recreating the Morrison myth. For a friend this should be welcome news. Don't believe it. I find very little truth in what I hear and read. What was once a simple and innocent question has become a debate and a labyrinth.

Throughout his life, the views of Jim were many and varied. In the April 1969 issue of *Life Magazine*, Fred Powledge wrote, "... he appears —in public and on his records—to be moody, temperamental, enchanted in the mind and extremely stoned on something. Once you see him perform, you realize that he also seems dangerous, which, for a poet, may be a contradiction in terms." Reporters provide instant analysis of what they perceive; unfortunately, they do not often reach beyond their first impressions. The public's perception of Jim Morrison was created from record company publicity releases and a few quickly rendered press reports.

When a journalist spent time with Jim, the results were often different. In 1969 Michael Cuscuna wrote in *Down Beat*, "In Jim Morrison, I found, to my surprise, a beautiful human being who has been a victim of sensational publicity and harassment by silly journalists. This same Jim Morrison seems trapped in the routine of success, with a public image to live up to, while his best musical and cinematic talents and ambitions remain stifled and/or untapped."

For close to three years I have been reading and rereading Jim's notebooks and journals to prepare his writings, especially his poetry, for publication. This irresistible contact with his work has given me a greater appreciation of his talent. I've found that Jim rarely penned

Frank Lisciandro, 1965. Opposite: Sometimes, when he stared into the lens, it was as if he was shedding layers of armour to reveal his vulnerability.

specific autobiographical notes about himself. Instead he applied his genius to the task of transforming events in his own life into universal observations. Even though I have become familiar with thousands of pages of Jim's handwritten text, I have uncovered few new clues to help me answer the question of who he was.

As the misinformation barrage about Jim increased, I noticed that the people who should be heard from—the people Jim trusted and worked with and tripped with and those he shared his time and thoughts with, his friends—were not being heard from at all. So I began to contact and interview Jim's friends one by one, hopeful that the questions I asked would elicit fresh information and significant insights.

It took time and effort to locate some of the people I wanted to talk with, while others searched me out, anxious to participate. Many had never been interviewed for publication before, and a few were reluctant to begin now. But I had this much going for me: everyone knew I was a close personal friend of Jim. They didn't view me as another reporter concocting a sensationalistic story, or an opportunistic outsider trying to pry loose long-hidden secrets. And with patience and generosity Jim's friends entrusted to me their memories and stories.

I have not included observations by Robby Krieger, John Densmore, and Ray Manzarek, the other members of The Doors. For more than twenty years they've been offered the opportunity to have their say, and I have not always agreed with them. These pages provide an opportunity for a different perspective on Jim, one that is not tainted by old rumors and myths. It's time to put aside what's been said in the past so that we can hear what Jim's friends have to say about him now.

There were two conditions I established for inclusion in *A Feast of Friends*: first, you had to have been one of Jim's friends (and I surely could not reach or include all of them); second, the people I interviewed could only relate, and I would only accept, what they saw and/or heard firsthand. I didn't want yarns whose origins were questionable or unreliable. In these pages, we always know the source for the information provided.

Everyone revealed what they saw and heard, yet this is basically a book of impressions and reflections. It is not science. It is not a set of answers. Human beings, especially if they are intense, creative, and powerful, cannot be pinned down under an easy label. Jim Morrison was never completely this or that, one way or another.

This book focuses on issues and occasions that illuminate an extraordinary human being. What we are searching for in all these clues and glimpses is a more accurate rendering, a more human and understandable portrait. By weighing the observations of those who knew Jim, we can reach our own conclusions about who he was and what his life meant. The pieces are provided; it is up to you to make the picture whole.

Opposite: Although he did not regularly smoke cigarettes, Jim developed a taste for cigars. Relaxing in a hotel room in Philadelphia after a concert, 1969.

Visions of a Concert

By the spring of 1966 it looked as if Jim's visions were about to come true.

This is not a biography; it doesn't attempt to follow Jim Morrison's life from the day he was born (December 8, 1943) to the day he died (July 3, 1971). Instead, it's a portrait drawn from multiple angles, each view complementing all the others. Don't feel you have to read the book by starting on page one. You won't get lost if you skip around and read chapters out of order. The book does have a structure, and the chapters are arranged roughly on a chronological time line, but each chapter is a separate view that can be read independent of the rest.

No matter where you begin, the following capsule history is intended as a road map to help you keep your bearings through the pages of anecdotes and remembrances.

In the late spring and summer of 1965 Jim Morrison was writing poems and songs and experiencing psychedelic visions of a concert in which he was singing his own songs before a vast audience. Later he said that the words and melodies he heard were as clear as any song on the radio.

One day, by chance, he ran into fellow UCLA film school graduate, Ray Manzarek; and The Doors were born. After eight months of rehearsals, personnel changes and repeated rejections by nightclubs and record companies, the band landed a steady job at the London Fog, a now-defunct club on the Sunset Strip. Their wages were almost nonexistent, but the club offered the band a space to perfect their material and obtain exposure in what was becoming a burgeoning LA rock scene.

By the spring of 1966 it looked as if Jim's visions were about to come true. The Doors were hired as the house band at the Whiskey a-Go-Go,

Jim and Pam having fun in a photo booth.

the premier club on the Strip, and before the end of the summer they had signed with Elektra Records and recorded their first album. Released in January 1967, *The Doors* made little impact on the music charts. But having an album released on an established label gave the band a chance to appear in better venues, and soon they were playing the fabled San Francisco ballrooms: the Avalon and the Fillmore.

Then in April, Elektra released an abbreviated version of "Light My Fire," a song from the first album. The song caught on and by the end of July it was No. 1 on the Billboard "Hot 100" survey. Now the album, with exposure from the single, shot up the charts. Heavy radio airplay and articles in major national magazines spread the band's popularity all over the country.

When their second album, *Strange Days*, was released in October it took only two weeks to hit No. 4 on the Billboard list. For the next few weeks both Doors LPs held positions in the Top 10, a rare and considerable achievement.

As their audience swelled, the group began appearing in large municipal auditoriums and sports arenas; and the quality of Jim's performance varied from night to night and city to city. His attempts to spontaneously create a psychic reaction in such vast spaces resulted in shows that were sometimes thrillingly brilliant and other times obvious and boring. On December 9, 1967 Jim was arrested on stage during a performance in New Haven, Connecticut; it was not the first nor the last of a series of bizarre encounters with the law.

Pictures of Jim appeared in magazines and newspapers; he was the new sex idol, and all over the country women vied for his attention. But only Pamela Courson possessed the subtle ingredients of intelligence, beauty, and allure to keep Jim coming back. They first met in 1967 when The Doors were playing at the London Fog, and through the years that followed, their romance, like a fire under siege from wind and rain, flickered and flamed bright.

The Doors' third and fourth albums did not have the critical appeal of the ground-breaking first two. Jim seemed less interested in performing and had no use for the privileged lifestyle that his fame and fortune bestowed. And despite the constant demands of touring and recording, he still found time to write. His notebooks show an unceasing

Jim came to abhor the bare-chested pretty boy image that he helped to create.

creative activity, a preoccupation with words and the development of a poetic craft. In everything he wrote he exhibited the wild flight of words characteristic of an artist caught up in spontaneous inspiration, while at the same time he displayed the care and patience of a craftsman refining a finished work.

He offered his poetry to the fan magazines and underground papers. In 1968 he self-published two books of his writings, *The Lords* and *The New Creatures,* and the following year they were combined and issued commercially under a single title.

What is most striking about Jim's writing is the attention to detail and the unswerving critical sensibility he brought to the practice of his craft. Because he viewed his written words as material in process, he could not resist making changes. He wrote and rewrote, each draft condensing the language, sharpening the rhythm, and pushing the poem a little closer to sinewy elegance.

On March 1, 1969, The Doors brought their show to a sweltering, overcrowded auditorium in Miami, Florida, and Jim's words and actions on stage touched off a storm of protest. Four days after the concert the local authorities filed a warrant for his arrest. The negative publicity forced the cancellation of more than twenty-five confirmed concert bookings. Radio stations in some parts of the country would not play Doors' songs. In Miami, "A Rally for Decency" drew more than thirty thousand to the Orange Bowl.

When The Doors could not tour because of the furor over Miami, Jim threw himself into other projects. He wrote, co-directed and acted in a film called *HWY*; he completed a screenplay with poet/playwright Michael McClure; he gave freely of his time and finances to the creation of Pamela's boutique "Themis." With the same energy that he pursued new projects, he hurried down the path of progressive alcoholism, consuming prodigious quantities of alcohol on a daily basis.

Morrison Hotel, The Doors' fifth LP, saw the band returning to a blues-inspired, good-time rock sound that captured many new fans and won praise from almost all the critics. Doors concert bookings picked up and Jim was once again bringing his version of rock theater to arenas in the United States, Canada, Mexico, and Europe. He grew a full and luxurious beard and gained weight. Some blamed the constant drinking; others said it was Jim discarding his rock idol image for the look of a street poet. And indeed he now seemed more determined than ever to establish himself as a serious poet. He recorded his poems with the plan of releasing a spoken word album separate from his activities with The Doors.

During the early months of 1971, Jim completed the vocals for the last album owed Elektra Records under their contract, and then he quietly slipped out of the United States to take up an extended residence in Paris, where Pamela had secured an apartment and was waiting for him. He hoped that he would find a quieter life in France so that he could devote time to writing and filmmaking.

Although he had left behind the bars and clubs he frequented in Los Angeles, he did not abandon the pleasure he found in alcohol. Paris afforded him more time to write, and judging by the few letters he wrote he seemed content and determined to stay.

Jim died in Paris on July 3, 1971, at the age of twenty-seven, and was buried in Pere Lachaise Cemetery. The death certificate listed the cause of death as heart failure.

Jim and Frank at the Lucky-U, a favorite bar and taqueria, on Jim's birthday in 1970.

An Allegory

I found it so incredible that a man could take this little event in his life where some idiot cop came and hit him in the eyes with Mace and turn it into an allegory...

When Vince Treanor, quiet, reserved, thirty-plus years old, saw The Doors perform at New Haven, Connecticut in 1967, he did not know that the experience would radically alter his life. *Before that concert, Vince would never have guessed that he would soon leap directly into the middle of rock 'n' roll and become an essential member of The Doors team.*

At that time I was an organ builder, had been for fifteen years, had quite a business going, had friends, family, a car: everything that I had was in this little town of Andover, Massachusetts.

I was into classical music and I was sort of an intellectual bent. I was listening to this popular music singularly because we had some kids working at the organ factory for the summer, and they would listen to the radio, and that was it. Believe me, it was not a thing of more or less choice, I got it sort of rammed down my throat, which was even more incredible, because when I heard The Doors' music, "Light My Fire" and "Crystal Ship," for the first time, I was stunned by the classicalness of that music.

A concert at the Hampton Beach Casino in August 1967 was Vince's first exposure to the band.

I came away from that show convinced that I had just seen the American Beatles. That I had seen the group that was going be the top group in the United States. I was impressed with the music, I was impressed with the orchestration, I was impressed with the delivery…it was just a very awesome experience, an electric…ah…it is an experience that cannot be described. You had to be there.

Above: Vince Treanor, 1969. Opposite: Jim on stage in New Haven, 1967.

Vince managed to attend a few more Doors concerts that summer and fall. Late in the year he and a few young friends traveled to New Haven to see The Doors again. It was December 9, 1967, the day after Jim's twenty-fourth birthday, and the first time Vince saw Jim up close. Vince had a good view of Jim and the events that were to unfold later that evening because he had access to the backstage area.

I had come down from Andover with four of my friends to see The Doors play. I had met Bill Siddons (*a nineteen-year-old college student who, at that time, was doing part-time work as The Doors' equipment manager and was to become, in a few months, their personal manager*) at several other concerts and would help him after the shows to pack up the equipment. So New Haven started out to be just another show. We had helped Bill put the equipment up, set it up, and then we were backstage when the alarm came, Jim's been Maced.

Jim had come to the New Haven Arena from dinner and found a girl in his dressing room and they began to talk. Since there wasn't enough privacy in the dressing room, Jim and the girl wandered away and found a shower stall (this was an arena where sporting events like hockey games were held, so in addition to the dressing rooms there were locker rooms and showers). Sometime later a member of the New Haven Police Department discovered the pair and asked them to move on. Jim, believing that they were being harassed, told the cop to fuck off. More words ensued. At some point in the confrontation the cop sprayed Mace in Jim's face causing chemical burns and temporary blindness.

Bill Siddons, 1970.

Bill Siddons and Ray Manzarek heard the news from a young boy who ran up to them yelling, "Your lead singer's been Maced." They reacted quickly, convincing the police that Jim was indeed their lead singer.

After he was Maced, Jim was taken out to a police car. The New Haven cops were about to drive him to jail when they realized that there were thousands of fans inside the arena expecting a concert. Taking Jim to jail might be a greater problem than letting him perform.

Ray and Bill helped Jim clean up. An apology from the police chief was made, and everyone thought that the unfortunate incident was over.

Jim had been Maced; he had been washed and bathed and anointed after the Macing, and was coming up onto the stage. He was a little tiddily, and thoroughly outraged at what had happened, although he appeared somewhat mollified by the apologies and backslapping of the police.

His face, of course, was still somewhat red and his eyes were still a little bit bloodshot, tearing a little bit. In his plight he sort of gave me a nod and went on upstage, 'cause at that point his mind was obviously preoccupied with other things.

*Biding his time onstage,
waiting to spring his surprise.*

After seeing Jim backstage Vince went out to the audience area. Meanwhile, on stage, Jim was back in control. For the audience of more than two thousand fans, Jim displayed his entire repertoire of moves. This is how Fred Powledge in Life Magazine *described it: "He stood before the six powerful amplifiers in his black leather pants and gyrated, sang, undulated, jumped, crouched, fondled, jerked, twisted, and projected poetry, at more than 1300 watts, into the old sports arena."*

Jim lived his life, but his stage life especially, with spontaneity. He took every moment as it came, and he dealt with it at that moment. He would play the audience. If the audience was hostile, he'd snap back at them. He could turn them on and off like a switch.

He would recite poetry, just bang, right off the top of his head. Or he would recite a piece of poetry which he'd written five years ago, but it just came to him and it moved him in that moment. And he would just come out with that, or he'd give a one-liner or a little dialogue. Ray, John, and Robby accompanied Jim. They were always backing him up, always following him. He would lead, he would give the direction, they would follow.

This silky, soft, but powerful voice, I don't know, it was like velvet, and at times made of steel. The dynamics, the range, the control he had.

The persona—I mean he would stand up there and he had this look on his face, and his eyes, those eyes, big, always dilated, you know? And you looked into them, and there was this hole and Morrison was in there, in that hole, that black hole. You couldn't touch it, you couldn't see it, but you knew that there was this mystery there, and whatever it was, you could hear it.

The last song he sang that evening, "Back Door Man," a blues number by Willie Dixon, has a chorus that seemed to be written with Jim in mind: "Well, the men don't know/ But the little girls understand."

At the beginning of a verse change in the song, Jim started a new riff, improvising lyrics to describe the events of the evening. "You want to hear a story? I'll tell you a story. Want to hear a story? It happened in this place, what's the name?"

"New Haven, New Haven," everybody's yelling "New Haven." And he tells them the story.

"I want to tell you about something that happened just two minutes ago right here in New Haven..."

The audience sat silent and listened while Jim improvised a monologue in time to the music. He related how he had had dinner and a few drinks, and how he had talked with a waitress about religion, and about arriving at the New Haven arena, and meeting a girl in his dressing room.

While the band played, Jim continued to improvise lyrics and what he sang piqued the interest of the police.

> And so we wanted some privacy
> And so we went into this shower room
> We weren't doing anything, you know,
> Just standing there and talking.
>
> And then this little man came in there,
> This little man, in a little blue suit
> And a little blue cap,
> And he said,
> "Whatcha doin' there?"
> "Nothin"
> But he didn't go away,
> He stood there
> And he reached 'round behind him
> And he brought out this little black can
>   of something...
> Looked like shaving creme,
> And then he
> Sprayed it in my eyes
> I was blind...

Opposite: Improvising the lyrics that would cause his sudden arrest.

Lt. Kelly, the ranking cop at the concert, tries to stop the show during the last verse of "Backdoor Man"

For Bill Siddons, Jim's improvised song was cathartic: a revelation of the split in American society: Youth versus Authority, one individual's rights versus the strong-armed tactics of the State.

BILL: Oh, it was fantastic. It was fantastic. It was like…I found it so incredible that a man could take this little event in his life where some idiot cop came and hit him in the eyes with Mace and turn it into an allegory for full reason to say "Fuck you!" to authority. And in the middle of "Back Door Man" he took a seven-minute break and related this whole story about his confrontation with the police. And he so humiliated the rationale of the police that he could have taken those thousands of kids and rallied them and they all would have died for him. It was unbelievable. That was such an incredible evening.

VINCE: The cops were furious that he had told this story. They thought they had made a pact. Everybody but Jim had said, "Yeah, it's all forgotten, it's cool." Jim just grinned. He would do things like that. Everybody around Jim would be saying, "Hey, that's cool, yeah, no problem, it's great." Jim just smiles. He doesn't say a word. So everybody would walk out with the impression that Jim was cool and it was okay.

But if you really thought about it, Jim hasn't said, he hasn't opened his mouth, he just smiled.

At the end of "Back Door Man," the lights suddenly came on as police appeared on the stage. Using the mic, Jim asked why the lights were on. There was no answer. "Do you want to hear one more?" he asked the crowd. In a united voice they shouted back, "YES!" "Then turn off the lights," Jim said, looking toward the light booth. "Turn off the fucking lights." Lt. Kelly, the ranking cop at the concert, appeared on stage, pausing for a moment, his hands on hips, frowning as if he were a cop in a play.

VINCE: He comes up, he walks up to Jim, comes up across the stage, puts his hand on the microphone and says, "You're under arrest. You're under arrest. This is the end of the show."

Jim pointed the mic at the cop and said, "Say your thing, man." One of the other cops on the stage grabbed the mic out of Jim's grasp. The audience was angry. More cops poured onto the stage.

VINCE: Jim was a consummate manipulator of crowds. He was incredibly good with that, he knew how to turn them on and off. He told them

Ray Manzarek advises caution, but Jim is determined to defy the police.

*Lt. Kelly informs
the audience that the
concert is over.*

the story and the crowd was on his side and then all of a sudden they saw this bust right before their eyes. He certainly did not deserve the treatment that he got and the kids knew it.

BILL: It was so ridiculous that twelve-year-old girls were yelling, "Fuck you, you stupid asshole," at the cops and saying obscenities that I hadn't even imagined yet. These little teeny girls, they didn't even have tits yet, were screaming at the police like this because Jim was absolutely irrefutable in his tale. He just told the truth. And you knew it was the truth. You knew this wasn't jive. That he had been mercilessly damaged because the police overreacted to a minor incident. And somehow he managed to tell this in the funniest little Southern drawl that he learned in Florida that made the cops look like absolute wimps without testicles. And so the police had to arrest him. I'm surprised he didn't get shot.

As the trouble on stage increased, Bill moved to protect Jim's body with his own.

BILL: When I was freaking out on the policeman, Jim looked at me and said, "Bill, you can't do anything. They have to do this. I'm going to jail. This is what's happening." And I looked at him, and he freed me from going straight out of my mind, 'cause he knew he had stepped over the line, and authority was now in charge. Not the authorities per se but people who were unable to overcome their programing.

VINCE: And two other cops come up and grab Jim, one on either side, and Jim has this ridiculous expression on his face and they turn him around and take him off, walking him through the curtain, down the steps at the back of the stage.

The kids in the audience were kind of stunned. I mean, the crowd was…I mean this was…shocking. First, to see the cops come up on stage and grab Jim. And it was a very abrupt end to an already somewhat controversial performance. And then they started to chant, and then the cops announce, "Okay, clear the building." You know, they swept the building out, got everybody out of the building. They were afraid of a riot. The audience, this conservative, New England audience weren't going to riot, they were just, "My God, what's going on?" It was really that, more than anything.

Vince and his friends made their way around the arena and managed to talk their way through the police lines by claiming to be part of the road crew. Arriving at the opening behind the stage, they witnessed Jim being led down the stage stairs by the cops.

VINCE: When he was taken down the stage —mind you, Jim is not a big guy, I mean he's a little heavier build than I am, but he's no buff California beach boy, let me tell you— and he was a pussycat anyway. He was a pacifist, if anything. And these two guys have got him. And no way he could even struggle.

Jim was taken off stage, he was taken down the steps, and as we arrived where the steps were, Jim was being held on the right and on the left by these two cops. The cop in front of him turned around and began to punch him in the face. Four times in the jaw with a balled fist. The guy actually hit him. The cop behind Jim was using his forearm, actually hitting Jim across the back and the lower neck and upper back with his forearm, sort of using the wrestler's forearm slam, pounding him across his shoulders and neck. About four or five times. We witnessed this.

I stood…I was probably eight to ten feet away, looking from the side. I mean we had a view of everything that was going on. Two cops holding him and of course Jim weighed 120 soaking wet. And these two big burly cops, one on either side, the one in front was doing the punching. Hit him four times…

Then they took him off. They actually took him out a side door, not the door where the truck would normally come in, but to a smaller side door where the parking lot was. A police car was waiting outside. That's where he was thrown to the ground and kicked.

I knew Jim was not a fighter but I also know that he was not a coward and I wondered if Vince had seen any sign of Jim trying to break free of the cops.

VINCE: He couldn't. There were two guys, one on each arm. Jim was turned around, taken down behind the stage, behind the curtain where nobody from the audience, or even anybody on stage, could see him at all. And it was there that they held him and the cop in front turned around and started to whack him in the face and the other guy started to pound his back.

Later they would claim he was resisting arrest.

VINCE: When Jim was taken off stage and the other Doors left, I said to Bill, "You gotta go, follow this guy down to the police station, do what you can do, but go. We'll take care of the stage." So me and my friends proceeded to pack up the equipment just moments ahead of the guys who were attempting to dismantle the stage under us. We rushed everything off, packed it up, loaded the truck, and went home.

In the lobby area of the arena, Tim Page, a combat-hardened photographer recently returned from Nam, photographed the police beating a teenage boy. One of the cops pushed Page out to the street. When Page protested the treatment and demanded an apology, he was promptly arrested. In quick succession the police arrested Yvonne Chabrier, a Life reporter and Michael Zwerin, a jazz critic whose articles appeared in The Village Voice. They were placed in a paddy wagon for the ride to the jail.

Jim was charged with breaching the peace, giving an indecent and immoral exhibition, and resisting arrest. The bail was $1500 and Bill Siddons posted the bond from the concert receipts, but he was not allowed to wait in the police station, not being a relative of the accused. He stood outside waiting in the cold New England December night wearing his California clothes, a T-shirt and cotton slacks.

VINCE: On the way home, we from New England, the staid, conservative, little town of Andover, couldn't believe that we'd actually seen our first incident of police brutality. Sunday night —the concert was Saturday— I called Bill and told him that…of course all this news had hit the newspaper, and we could see that there was going to be trouble, so I said, "Hey, Bill, tell the attorneys that if they want to file a suit or countercharge against the police, we will go into court."

When this whole thing subsided, the charges against Jim were dropped. Most likely because they didn't want the Mace incident to come out in court, which it would have.

During that phone call Bill then told me that because he was missing so much school, he was going to lose his draft deferment, so he would have to be leaving the band. He said, "I can't continue with the group. If you want the job, call the manager." Which I did on Friday morning, and by noon we made an arrangement and they set up a first-class ticket and I went American Airlines to San Francisco on December 26.

Was I nervous? I left my mother and father, my sister and my brother, my business, my car, my friends…I spent five hours on that plane going through the greatest crisis of my life. Did I do the right thing? Will I make it? Can I handle this? Will the guys like me? Am I going to be able to…I mean every minute I was getting further and further away from home and the security of thirty-odd years to be hurled into an unknown: no friends, no acquaintances, nothing. I had nothing out there at all. I mean I was a stranger in a strange land.

I met the band at Bill Graham's Fillmore West, actually Winterland, and my second meeting with Jim was auspicious, he threw me out of the dressing room. He said, "Would you mind leaving?" He didn't know who I was.

Jim Morrison would come to know and count on Vince Treanor to provide the behind-the-scenes technical support for the band's powerful stage sound. Vince stayed with the band until the end, never missing a concert, always there with a spare part or a screwdriver when a key component broke down. He says he's never regretted leaving his other life behind.

With his long hair and angular features, Vince was often mistaken for a member of The Doors. Here he is with Jim in New York, 1969.

Beatniks

We wanted to get on the road and travel, and go taste beer in Mexico, and see if we could pick up women in France.

Well this is it, 1717 Alameda Ave. Jim Morrison lived here when he was thirteen and fourteen years old, in 1957 and '58. Jim had control of that round room up there and on rainy days and days when we didn't feel like doin' anything this is where we'd hang out, where we'd do sketches and come up with ways to trick people. It was kind of like the attic away from the parents and everyone else, nobody messed with it...

I was standing on a quiet, tree-shaded street in Alameda, California looking up at a tall, well-made Queen Anne style house. At my side, Jim's boyhood friend, Fud, pointed out the room where they'd pass the time.

Jim was thirteen years old when he met Fud Ford during the first weeks of the ninth grade at Alameda High School. The Morrisons— Commander Steve, mom Clara, younger sister Ann and kid brother Andy— moved to Alameda, an island adjacent to Oakland, when the Navy reassigned the Commander. It was 1957 and rock 'n' roll was making strong inroads into American popular culture. Elvis was already crowned the King, and every week millions watched Ricky Nelson play guitar and sing on his parents' popular TV series, "The Adventures of Ozzie and Harriet."

Whoever Jim's close friends were before he landed in Alameda, it's doubtful that they could have matched Fud's combination of wit, street smarts and recklessness. We talked at a popular record shop where Fud is both manager and resident expert on all things musical from the fifties and sixties.

I'm a local boy that he found when he first moved to town to help show him the ropes, and we ended up being really good friends. He was exactly my age and I had a good base of friends built up, and so I introduced him to my gang of friends. People really liked him. He knew

Fud Ford, a year or so after Jim left Alameda.

how to get along with people, from moving around I suppose, and he was really good at it.

We were together most of the time. In high school you have one guy that you hang out with mostly and it just happened to be me.

Before arriving in Alameda, Jim had moved often as his father climbed through the ranks of Navy hierarchy. Children who move frequently become loners because, the theory goes, they would rather stand alone than endure repeated separations from new-found friends.

Fud was shaking his head.

Nah, he was exactly the opposite; he was really friendly. I think he liked movin' around 'cause he'd meet new people; new people to joke around with and pull practical jokes on. That's what first attracted me to him. He got in one of the classes that I had and his sense of humor was just...just tremendous.

And Jim was a pretty good athlete, a member of the Alameda High School swim team, good enough to make the team and compete in the events as a freshman. He was real good at the butterfly, which is a real hard stroke that takes a lot of upper body muscle. And he had a lot of upper body strength, his shoulders and arms were well developed.

NAKED FUN

Writers and poets start somewhere. Was Alameda, with its views of the Bay Bridge and San Francisco skyline, inspiration for the young Jim Morrison?

No, the only thing I'd see him write were inane little comedy routines that he'd perform for people unlucky enough to call his phone number by accident or phone their house. He'd answer the phone in a black voice, "Ah this here's Thelma," or an oriental voice, "Mollisons lesidence." Different accents. He was definitely into theater.

He had access to the Navy facilities. They had a wrestling room with mats, and we'd go in there and wrestle around. We put together a routine that we'd do and it would look like we were really street fighting. We'd roll around the street in front of a bus and make the bus stop and throw one another around.

And at the swimming pool he'd walk along the ledge and, you know, make it look like he would fall into the water. And he did the same thing on the diving board: walk out on the diving board, catch his foot, stumble and pretend like he'd fallen off. And he'd get "oh's" and "ah's" from the people sitting around, and traumatize old ladies. All that stuff he did later on when he was a superstar, walking out on the twentieth story ledge of hotels. He perfected his riff here in Alameda, he was a real show-off.

The quiet moments of contemplation were more like moments of planning and plotting on what to do, who to play a practical joke on next and how to do it. He was really good at practical joking, real good.

Here in Alameda every street goes down to a beach. Every street on the south shore had its own private beach and in the summer you'd just go down there in your swimming suit and it's really easy to doff 'em and run around flipping off the city with one hand, holding your trunks with the other, just yukkin' it up. We had a lot of fun, you know, just fun, naked fun.

Did Jim carry his love of jokes and pranks into the high school?

Oh, yeah. He'd get ticketed by the hall patrols that they had for going up the wrong stairway, or just laying down pretending he was dead right in the hallway between class breaks and people would have to walk around him.

Whenever he could, he'd quip the teachers. He spent a lot of time in detention and in the principal's office.

Although he was smaller than his teammates, Jim was a powerful swimmer and made the junior varsity swim team his first year at Alameda High School. Jim signed his name in Fud's yearbook.

Were there any teachers that you guys liked?

I don't remember having any good teachers. I'm sure they were there but I considered high school pretty much a waste of time. I think most kids did and still do. Jim was probably as smart as most of his teachers. Extremely smart. With a modicum of effort he got really good grades. We'd take school pretty lightly.

What about fights and rumbles, that Rebel Without a Cause kind of thing that we associate with growing up in the fifties?

I don't remember him getting into any fights or being violent at all, even to the point of getting mad. I don't even remember him ever getting mad.

Drugs weren't popular yet and as far as drinking, we were at the learning stage. Drinking was acceptable; you went out and drank with your fraternity buddies on the weekends. We'd occasionally have a taste of the Commander's private brew, but not much.

OUT WITH A BANG

Larry Keenan, another local Alameda kid, remembers being in several high school classes with Jim. But Larry's circumstances were very different than Fud's:

LARRY: Fud and I went to St. Joseph's School, which is a Catholic grammar school, but I wasn't able to cruise the streets of the city, little island actually, like Fud was able to. So Fud probably knew a lot more people that we called "the public school kids" because he was out a lot more, he was on the street most of the time actually. And he got in a lot of trouble, even when we were little kids.

At Alameda High Larry had the opportunity to observe Jim's antics up-close.

LARRY: I wasn't someone who hung out with Morrison, but I did get to watch him some. You could actually feel something in his presence. You knew he had something. You knew there was a magic around him—that's probably the word you'd use. There was just something that everybody seemed to recognize. Everybody was always talking about him, what he did here and what he did there. I would come home and talk about him to my family and to my brothers and sister. He was just a unique kind of person, somebody you would tell stories about just because he would just do these outrageous kinds of things.

He was the kind of guy that could get away with being a jerk, and people liked him for it. I mean, it wasn't just the kids, it was the teachers too, because the teachers didn't shoot him down that much. It's this magic that he had. I mean, everybody knew he was screwing up or they knew he was kind of a jerk, but nobody called him on it. That was the part that always amazed me. Cause my parents were so strict, I was used

to being beaten down for something like that, and I was watching this guy, day in and day out, get away with this stuff. And nobody else was getting away with it.

If he got called on in class, he always had a good answer. And that's the other half of it. The fact that it wasn't just his actions, but that he was a mouth, and he could get away with it. There was just a way that he could say something to somebody that was outrageous and he wouldn't get busted for it, while another person saying the exact same thing would. He just had a better way of putting it, or he was just weirder about it.

And he was very funny. I don't remember him telling jokes as much as I remember him just being outrageous. He'd be the one, you know, with the comment about the class and everyone would laugh. He was loud, so he was very disruptive in class, sure, but he was really funny, oh yeah.

The imposing facade of Alameda High must have impressed Jim on his first day of classes. In time, he made the school his stage.

How did Jim get to be that way?

LARRY: This was rebel times, you know, James Dean time. And I think that was part of it. Him being the son of a military officer. And I knew many of these kids myself. They hate the regimentation and the rigidity and all of it, and they're looking for something else to do. And I think that Morrison, he was just…he was just coming unglued. I mean he was just outrageous. That's what everybody remembers about him, his incredible energy, just to be outrageous. And I think someone like Fud, who was outrageous already in his own right and just a total non-conformist, probably really helped.

On his last day in Alameda, Jim planned to leave his fellow students with something they could talk about long after he was gone.

LARRY: Someone from the principal's office came into the class. They just came in and said it was time for him to go. He had to leave right in the middle of class. Jim, he said, "Well, I want to go out with a bang," and he walked up and put a firecracker on the edge of the teacher's desk, lit it, hung around a few seconds and walked out, walked right out the door. And that was how he left.

MAD MAGAZINE & THE BEAT POETS

Young kids, when asked by their parents and grandparents, usually say that when they grow up they're going to become astronauts or cops or super heroes. By junior high other realities begin to take hold and dreams change. What did Jim and Fud see for themselves as a career?

FUD: We wanted to be beatniks like the characters in *On the Road*. We wanted to get on the road and travel, and go taste beer in Mexico, and see if we could pick up women in France. Just mostly fantasies: what turned out to be fantasies for me, reality for him. Reading *On the Road* was great for a young mind to fantasize about. These guys were just out there doin' it, and livin' life to the fullest.

And that was when the beatnik days were happenin'. We'd put on sweatshirts and Levis and wear sandals and go over to San Francisco, to North Beach and hang out, you know, hang about in front of the coffeehouses or go in and listen to the poetry sometimes. Try and steal wine. Spend time out at Playland at the beach, that was a great place to have fun for a kid. Gone now.

So Jim was reading the beat writers.

FUD: He read everything from *Mad Magazine* to the beat poets and novelists of the time. Instead of listening to rock 'n' roll records he'd read Kenneth Rexroth and stuff like that.

Opposite: Jim's pencil sketch, a caricature of a beatnik, is one of the drawings and cartoon cutouts that Fud managed to save.

Are you telling me that Jim ignored rock 'n' roll?

FUD: Oh, we'd listen to music, but when he'd listen to rock 'n' roll chances are it would be Elvis. He really liked Elvis. But more often than not we'd listen to records, it would be comedy records or spoken word records. Ferlinghetti and Rexroth both had albums on Fantasy Records.

Listening to poetry records does sound a little strange, but it's true. You could go to Stairway to Music in Oakland. They had a big section of that kind of stuff, so we didn't have to go too far. I was into R 'n' B and so we'd go to Duo Records and get stuff for me and up to Stairway and get stuff for him.

POT & WHORES

According to Fud, Jim wasn't writing poetry and except for Elvis he wasn't listening to much rock 'n' roll. I was almost afraid to ask about girls.

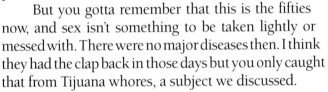

FUD: Yeah, oh yeah, he was popular with everybody but especially girls. He didn't have a steady girlfriend. Lot of girls liked him and during the summer we'd spend time going to different girls' houses, using 'em as much as possible for food and entertainment.

But you gotta remember that this is the fifties now, and sex isn't something to be taken lightly or messed with. There were no major diseases then. I think they had the clap back in those days but you only caught that from Tijuana whores, a subject we discussed.

And where did these two guys, just barely in their teens, get the material to discuss border town prostitutes?

Jack Kerouac…

Of course.

…reading his book, *On the Road*, these guys travel to Mexico and they talk about pot and whores, so we always fantasized about that…fucking whores.

MESS AROUND

Fud hung out at the Morrison house and was on friendly terms with Jim's mom and dad.

FUD: Jim's mother, Clara, was…she was a regular mom. As I remember now, she'd be considered a really good mother. I remember her at the sink with her apron on, and takin' care of the three kids. She was pretty nice. She was strict. She always made Jim comb his hair and wear clean clothes when in those days you were really cool if you didn't wash your Levis. Your Levis would stand in the corner by themselves after they got ripe. She couldn't see this as a fashion statement; she only saw it as dirty pants and made Jim wear clean ones. But he totally forgot all of it as soon as he walked out the door.

Jim's father, oh you knew he was important and not a man to be messin' around with. He just sorta commanded respect when he walked into a room. He was a career military man; Jim called him the Commander. And to me he seemed to be a kind of an absentee father, he wasn't around a whole lot. Jim didn't talk about him very much.

We'd hang around drawing, listening to the radio and records, I dunno, I think it was pretty normal. Just hang around. My house was good. We could pretty much do whatever we wanted at my house. His house we escaped up into the attic and just messed around. You mess around when you're a kid.

WHEELIES

The Slaymaker family lived next door to the Morrisons; Richard Slaymaker was the same age as Jim and Fud.

I had known Richard since the third grade and he was dying of leukemia and we'd go over and try and cheer him up and talk to him and stuff. We'd visit him virtually every day. Jim would say or I'd say, "Let's go say hello to Richard."

We went over there for six months or so. Cheer him up, just like visiting, only it was real easy to do, he was right there, just next door.

He was in a wheelchair and they'd wheel him out and put him in the sun and we'd wheel him around, do wheelies with him. He couldn't go to school; he was purple. They don't let purple guys in school. They don't allow that around here.

He started going pretty fast toward the end. Then he died.
I don't remember going to the funeral or anything, but we'd seen him deteriorate and turn different colors.

I could tell it was sad for Jim, because Richard was dyin' and it was sort of Jim's idea to go over all the time and try and cheer the guy up. He had great compassion.

MOVING AGAIN

After living in Alameda for less than two years, the Morrisons moved again.

They were goin' to Norfolk, Virginia. The Commander had been promoted to Captain and was getting his first commission.

Oh, it was a very sad experience for me. And Jim, he was saddened by it too. I was losing my best friend and so our last time together was at my house. I can remember the Commander driving up. They had a really ugly, turquoise Packard, and they picked him up and drove my best friend away. It was really sad. One of the few times I cried when I was a kid.

*The young Jim Morrison and his buddy Fud concocted their practical jokes
in the dormer room at the top of this house in Alameda.*

Little Brother

...he asked me one time when we were alone, he says, "Well, have you ever broken through?" And I answered him, "Yes." Because I had. I definitely had.

Throughout his life Jim chose companions that had to test and explore that thin stretch of territory between acceptable behavior and disturbing the peace. Jim met Philip O'Leno in 1964 at the UCLA film school where they were both undergraduate students dreaming about becoming filmmakers. Philip, who had studied acting at Los Angeles City College, was tall, moody, and well read. His inspiration was Orson Wells, the brilliant, young director of Citizen Kane and Touch of Evil.

Philip O'Leno, at work on a UCLA student film production, 1965.

When I first met Jim, he was simple. High energy. Intelligent. A lot of fun. Unsophisticated. Not that I was so sophisticated in the ways of the world. He was only a year or two younger, but he was my little brother. That was the kind of relationship we had.

I would give him lectures, like a big brother would, you know. Not "how to run your life" lectures. No, no, just things in the way of the world. He was very strong and dynamic and self-assured. He just hadn't been around much; he had more of a sheltered life, I guess. So that's what I mean by simple: he'd hadn't been exposed to much of the outside world.

Two guys in particular I took up with, besides Jim, were Ray Manzarek and John DeBella. And we sort of gravitated together. Jim came along with me. I sort of take credit for having...It doesn't mean much, but, I did, I brought them together.

When Philip brought Jim and Ray together, he forged a link that would eventually lead to the founding of The Doors. But at that moment it wasn't rock 'n' roll Jim Morrison was thinking about, it was film.

DIRTY MOVIE

Like me he had this calling. He wanted to be a filmmaker. It was an ultimate art. Back then we spent days on end, months, refining and defining our film theories.

We shared a club of attitudes about films and the history of film and dedication to the craft. And those who had it more were those who hung together more.

Once you had acquired the basic filmmaking skills, it was time to apply those techniques in a real film of your own.

In the psychology department, they were running films to subjects in a chair with all of their responses monitored. The galvanic skin response, and brain waves and heartbeat. Totally wired. To see what certain images would do to them. Well this was just my field. Jim thought it was far out too.

Through persistence, and with the help of one of his cinema professors, Philip was hired to make films for the psychology department research.

I made three films. One was called *Melancholia*. Let's bypass the second one, I can't even remember what it was. The third one was *Sexuality.*

We didn't do anything, really. We went to a friend's beach house and an actor friend of mine, he took his girlfriend. And they took off their clothes. Everything except their underwear. And we just got in close. Various skin shots of a couple caressing in the afternoon. But no fucking.

Well, Jim saw this footage and he said, "Wow! This is great, man! Can I have some of this?" I said, "Sure. Take it. I don't care." This was the stuff that I'd already rejected, put in a bag to be thrown away. And he cut it together and made his own film.

He just cut the footage really fast, so it looked like there was a lot more going on. A lot more going on than was going on. Because there wasn't anything even in all the dailies....But, that would be like him, to make a controversy out of something that he could use.

It caused quite a furor at the showing. Everybody was screaming at him. Especially all the faculty. Do you know the one I'm talking about? This "dirty movie" that he made?

I wish I could say yes, but I don't remember a single projected image from Jim's film. Nor do I recall Jim talking about it, or about the other films he made at UCLA. It was as if a door would shut the instant after an event occurred and he would move on to the next episode unfolding in his life.

He was a mischievous person. And the joke was, and it was known then, that those were just outtakes from the film I had done for the psych department, which they locked away in their vault. A totally harmless little thing. They wanted some kind of arousal, for the purpose of science, but they didn't want any kind of arousal. I don't know what they had in mind.

When I mention that he was Jim's closest friend during the years they were both at UCLA, Philip demurs.

Well, I don't know. At some times, certainly. But he stuck pretty much to himself.

We would call each other up, you know, various times of the night and read some new writing. I'd call him up from the library and get off on some really far-out, you know, subconscious stuff, mythological, Jungian... I'd call him up and read the whole thing. He'd point out what was good and what was bad. He'd say, "Oh yeah, that's good. What about such and such?"

So, I don't know. Knew him well. Knew each other. Loved each other.

A photo duel. Jim wields his new super 8mm movie camera, while Paul Ferrara aims his Nikon.

JUMPED OFF THE EARTH

The summer of 1965 was a magical one for Jim. In June he graduated from UCLA but declined to attend the ceremony. He cut communications with his family, moved out of his apartment, and began living wherever someone would find him a spare bed, or a spare couch, or even a spare corner to sleep in. He didn't have a car, nor any more possessions than he could carry. A few friends opened their doors to Jim, and when he ran out of friends there were the rooftops of Venice and a canopy of stars. It was the summer of change, of metamorphose.

> **Metamorphose. An object is cut off from its name, habits, associations. Detached, it becomes only the thing, in and of itself. When this disintegration into pure existence is at last achieved, the object is free to become endlessly anything.**
>
> *(from* The Lords*)*

A chance encounter that summer between Jim and Ray Manzarek, at a time when each was looking for an outlet for their creative energies, led to the idea of the The Doors. But, as Philip remembers, the band was not Jim's primary concern after the summer ended.

Well, getting high was…you know. Getting high and transcending. If he could have jumped off the earth then, he would have, without the music. But music was obviously the way to do it. And he and Ray knew it. Ray would say, "Well, we're going to be the last of the great bands. First it was The Byrds and then The Doors. And that's the end of it." And we all knew that without having to question it or wonder. Sure enough, that's the way it came to be.

But Jim would have gone off if somebody had appeared: somebody with magic. Or if some situation had manifested itself. But this band was what he was supposed to do. To get the basis for which he could work, and be heard. He got high just by being on stage. I mean he got into places where few people get to go. He and the band, too.

I had said to Jim, when John DeBella and I were leaving for Mexico, I said, "Why don't you come go with us." He says, "No, I think LA looks pretty good to me right now. I think there's things happening here, I'm not going to go anywhere." This was when we were just getting out of school.

For him, you know, things were happening. You know how you have the feeling of destiny in front of you, he had that sense.

Jim was a spontaneous radical and never felt compelled to follow any of the gurus or holy men that were so much a part of the lifestyle of the sixties.

I mean he might not meditate or go into a church but he always tried to, I'm speaking of the days I knew him, to treat everyone fairly and

On stage in Los Angeles, late 1967

honestly…no shit or misunderstandings or bad vibes or anything. That's a very spiritual place.

And if in my behavior, I wasn't maybe treating someone, what might be the better way, then little brother would correct me or remind me. He could see…he had a very old soul. He was immature but he could see.

BROKEN THROUGH

On May 4, 1953, when Jim Morrison was nine years old, Aldus Huxley drank down a glass of water containing mescaline crystals. For Huxley it was like "…what Adam had seen on the morning of creation." In the spring

---

of the following year he published a small book about the experience, The
Doors of Perception. *The title was borrowed from an observation of William
Blake: "If the doors of perception were cleansed every thing would appear
to man as it is, infinite."*

*Huxley's book sold steadily to a new generation anxious to change the
mind set of the fifties. In the early 1960s Timothy Leary and Richard Alpert
of Harvard University began publishing their research into the effects of
psychedelic drugs. Within a year, LSD from the Swiss pharmaceutical
company Sandoz, and from home labs on the East and West coasts filtered
onto college campuses. Before October 1968 possession and ingestion of
LSD might have been considered dangerous, but it was perfectly legal
almost everywhere in the United States. Jim used the drug early and often.*

We got very high. We got very high. You know there's moments
there when miracles happen, miracles taken for granted because there
just isn't any other way to relate to them. Miracles of life, energy, great
synchronicity, you might say, the way things happen, you know, all laid
out. It's enough to make not just the Almighty but the All more evident
to everyone pursuing it.

In other words, Jim wasn't doing this strictly for fun, whatever he
was doing, it wasn't just for high. It was for a true transcendental space
to arrive at. Which, I would say on stage, evolved. You know, it's giving
and taking that got him off and got his audiences off. But you can't do
that all the time.

After I got back from Mexico and I had that place on Third Street
in Santa Monica, he asked me one time when we were alone, he says,
"Well, have you ever broken through?" And I answered him, "Yes."
Because I had. I definitely had. Some of the experiences I had on
mushrooms up there in the mountains, I was completely transcended
out. I no longer…I was cut off completely from physical life and I was
bound up in the experience completely.

Did you and Jim take many psychedelic trips together?

More than I can remember. And no bad experiences, none whatever. Nor for myself. You know, the openness and the freeness and the lack of fear cause that not to happen. With a bad trip, I don't know, people have things all tied up inside of them or are afraid. No bad trips, nothing at all. Funny drugs, but no bummers.

We would walk on walls, on fences, I mean…overhanging ledges from buildings, and things like that, for the fun of it, but it was thrilling because we'd be on acid, and it really tuned us in.

Thrill-taking…it'd be late at night in the canals in Venice, and we'd deliberately play hide and seek with each other. We'd get lost from one another tripping, and then have to telepath where the other was. We'd be blocks away from each other but we'd have to always end up at the same spot without any prior arrangements. That was fun. That was a thrill.

Philip believes that transcendence was not the purpose of The Doors, but that it was a message that Jim wanted to make his audience aware of.

The breaking on through is what that's about. Like he asked me in that apartment on Third Street, "Have you ever broken through?" He wanted to know if I really had. I said, "Yes." And I was thinking of some of my mushroom experiences where I had totally gone all the way out and been shown by spirit guides the way around. And come back. I said, "Yes."

That's what that meant for him. Not just drugs. But a way of breaking out of the shell, and becoming another being. To die and to be born again.

And had Jim broken through at the time of that 1965 conversation?

He said, "I haven't." But then, remember when he said that to me the band hadn't really got going yet. Later he would. Probably on stage. I mean Jim was free, with the band at his back, he could just go out anywhere with an audience. Powerfully. You don't have to be alone to do it. So, I'm convinced that he did.

WANDER AND WANDER

The itch of adventure and the need to break out and do something made Jim and Philip restless. Night after night, without a destination, they would jump into Philip's car and drive.

Just to drive and meet other people. Go to somebody's house, be on the road, smoking. Mostly smoking. Take a trip somewhere and we'd land in all kinds of…half the time we knew the people, half the time we didn't. Just to drive.

Los Angeles, 1968.

We went down to downtown LA a lot. Sometimes we'd go see the strip shows which were pretty interesting at that time. And "three big hits 50 cents", that bought you a lot of classic films. We'd wander and wander around downtown.

We avoided the law like the plague. But we did it in the Bob Dylan sense: "If you live outside the law, you must be honest." So anything we did was openly and honestly, not flagrantly, but just openly, whatever we did. And just leave us alone, you don't want anything to do with us. Because I'm not disturbing the peace, just stay away.

BEAT TO A PULP

See Felix (*another film school cohort*) and Jim and I, we were getting a little bit crazy, the three of us. Too crazy. So it was difficult for the band, The Doors, to rehearse really. Jim would rather get fucked up. Anyway, Felix and he and I left, to go to the desert to get high, find some Indians, eat some peyote. Actually it was right after New Year's, so it would have been around January of '66.

But, meanwhile, Felix had brought some Sandoz (*LSD made by Sandoz Labs*) and he wanted to take it now. I wasn't really into it; I didn't want to take any acid there. I wanted to go and get on to where we were going. So, we had taken a room somewhere on the state line, and Felix brought out the acid and then we walked up an arroyo and that's where I lost them.

Before that there was a moment in that motel we rented, before we had gone out, when Jim took this check and lit it with a match. Didn't say a word to us, we were both very interested in what was going on.

And he holds the check up to burn, turns it over in his fingers until it's finished burning, in the way he has of doing things. I know there's a check, but that's all I can tell. And I assume it's from his parent. I think it was a point of real rejection. You got to remember that his father was commanding an aircraft carrier and this is happening during the Viet Nam war.

And so…and anyway, we parted there around Needles, California. I went on into Arizona. And they turned back to the city. At that point they were hitchhiking. And the following year in New York, Jim told me that they got a pretty good beating on the way back. The two of them were beat to a pulp. A bunch of guys, rednecks, descended on them. I never saw Felix again. He died a year before Jim.

THE END

Philip was gone for months, first to Arizona, then on to Mexico and then New Orleans and New York. When he returned he heard good news about his friends.

Someone said to me, "The Doors are playing at the London Fog, you ought to go by and hear them." I thought about it. And I decided not to, as much as it would be nice to hear them. And to see Jim again. But, that parting on the desert was truly the end. That was it.

I had made my decision. And I didn't go to see them. I left LA for New York. So you know the lyrics of the song, "End of nights we tried to die",

The Doors perform at The Scene, New York City, June 27, 1967.

and "I had to set you free, you would not follow me?" When The Doors came to New York in the winter of 1967, I asked Jim about that song, "The End", and when he had written it. He grinned, you know like he used to do, and said, "Oh, right about the time you split for New York."

Well, of course, friends follow one another basically, one's on and then the other's on, pretty much it grows that way. Well, I couldn't go on his trip. And he couldn't go on mine, because he had work to do. He had the work of his music. It's just as well I wasn't around to distract him. So, that's what the farewell was all about.

Waiting to board another plane, 1968.

33A

We had missed the scheduled flight out of New York City for the performance in Saratoga Springs. Bill reached into his bag of tricks and chartered a plane for Jim and the film crew. Left to right: a taxi driver, Paul Ferrara, an airport employee, Jim, John DeBella, and Bill Siddons.

→ 35A   → 36

Controlled Chaos

He wanted to push anything to the limit. Just like when he was walking on the edge of the ledge. He wanted to see how far far was.

*O*ver twenty years had passed since I had last seen January, and at first I did not recognize the handsome, smiling man that opened the door to the house on a hill across the bay from San Francisco. But when he said my name, his voice, deep and assured with that hint of an attitude, I knew who it was, and that he had not changed.

January is totally spontaneous and without pretension; it's easy to see why Jim found him a friend. They were carefree daredevils who loved thrills, words, women, good food, booze, and having fun. They both wanted to be boys again, and discovered that the spirit and freedom of the sixties allowed them to get away with almost anything.

The master of several trades—chef, carpenter, clothes designer, jeweler—January was already a successful longhaired entrepreneur when he hooked up with Jim.

January Jansen, 1968.
Opposite: Hollywood Bowl, 1968.

We met in a bar in Santa Monica, on the boardwalk, the late part of the summer, the summer that he'd finished school, 1965. And there was a bunch of sailors in there and Jim was sitting there drinking, as I was too, both of us drinking shots of tequila. We turned and looked at each other and said, "Hey." I guess there was comfort in numbers, because everybody else in there was a skinhead.

He looked like the same innocent, impish little boy that was always full of trouble, as he did throughout his life. He was always very polite—a gentleman, up to a point—and then, as it later came out by his own words, what he really, really was into was controlled chaos.

He said, "Hey, let's get outta here and see if we can find something cute." Jim was telling me that he had been writing poems and was

thinking about putting them into songs, and making some music. Neither one of us were really living anywhere, we were just kind of bouncing around. Stay a few nights here, stay a few nights there.

JEKYLL & HYDE

One time we were taking a trip. We started out at my place in the city, and we took off down Highway 1, through Big Sur. And Jim was writing poetry as we were going along. And that's where that verse, "The mansion is warm at the top of the hill..." comes from.

> **The mansion is warm at the top of the hill**
> **Rich are the rooms and the comforts there**
> **Red are the arms of luxuriant chairs**
> **And you won't know a thing till you get inside**

> (*from* "Not to Touch the Earth")

That came into his notebook as we went by Hearst Castle. And every place that there was a gas station, a motel, or a restaurant, we would stop so Jim could call Pamela and give her the latest verse out of the book of poems. And Paul and Babe, who were traveling with us, they'd say, "Ah. He's unreal, he's got it bad." But he would never admit it.

We wound up down the coast in a trailer of this friend of mine in Lime Kiln Canyon. And we're rocking around in the trailer and a song of his comes on. In fact, it was "The Crystal Ship", and it didn't hit him right at the time. That song always used to bother him whenever it'd come on the radio. Then it was like, "Why are they playing it now, at this time?" Whatever time of day or night it was, it was the wrong time. He was embarrassed listening to his voice. Just the shyness that would creep over him every now and then.

And he turned—he was the classic Jekyll and Hyde—turned around and spun into this spasm. And as he did, the trailer rocked off its blocks. It was a two-wheel trailer on blocks and it tipped. It was an interesting evening.

We bounced right back the next morning and headed on down the coast. And again, we still had to stop at every gas station and every motel and every liquor store, every place, anyplace that had a pay phone, so he could call Pamela and read her the latest from his notebook.

Opposite: Jim on stage in Columbia, Maryland, August 1968.

LIZARDS & SNAKES

I used to make his clothes. He said he wanted something in leather but didn't like what was available. Everything looked…what was it he said? He said, "It looked like linoleum." Most of the leather clothing that was out looked like linoleum, and he wanted something that made him look like a lizard and a cowboy.

In 1966 and1967 Jim and January were often mistaken for brothers.

Above: One of January's creations.

One of the interesting things about making his clothes was that I didn't have to go through cuts and fittings. If it would fit me, it would fit him. Except when it got to a point where he drank more beer than I did and I had to make certain adjustments.

One day, we were talking and walking down Santa Monica Boulevard and he said, "You know? I'd like to have a snakeskin suit." To go along, I guess, with his fascination and intrigue with lizards and snakes. And I said, "I can make one for you." And he says, "Yeah, right." Then I made him a snakeskin suit. And then I was condemned for a period of years to repair the thing.

I made all the black leather. And I was constantly remaking the snakeskin pants, because they were having a problem here or there or he fell in the ocean. And I did linen shirts and velvet shirts with embroidery.

PERFORMANCES

There was a time at the Fillmore West. At the time it wasn't even called Fillmore West, because it was the original Fillmore. That's when The Doors were still playing two sets a night. And Jim…it was not a drug-induced stupor, and it was not a booze-induced stupor. It was Jim, and on Jim's level of intensity, working on that message that he was wanting to get out there. It went beyond the music. He'd turn around and spin around, and he let go of the mic cable. And he was spinning it. Spinning this mic cable around and around and letting it out. He was picking up this "Whoosh!" This eerie sound was, to him, playing the music that he wanted to get into. And he turned around and spun and fell off the stage into the light panel down below. And the bulbs were going off just like flashbulbs, crashing and sparking. And when he came back up on stage, he'd lost his shirt. Some little girl had run off with his shirt. So, I took my jacket off and gave him my shirt. Just put my jacket back on.

His performances were more intense than audiences were ready for and they would come away from it, for the most part, very starry-eyed flower children. And some of them were like, "Whoa," and the others would come away and they didn't really know what they heard, or what they were asked. Because Jim's music at the time wasn't so much what the audience was hearing. It was what he was asking them.

Jim and January hanging out with fans before a concert in San Jose, California, 1968.

He was asking them to come along on a journey. Come along and be free. Come along and grow and run with him. And turn things around.

One of the things Jim couldn't handle was the popularity, the people clinging to him. And it was not because of anything other than the fact that he didn't know how to weigh it; whether it was real sincere in respect and in thirst for the poetry and the message, or whether it was, in fact, part of the groupie throngs, because that was part of the scene then.

Yeah, the popularity embarrassed him. He knew that he wasn't getting through to people on the one level that he wanted and that on the other level, he was coating everybody with this celebrity status. He felt uncomfortable, very uncomfortable.

On stage in the snakeskin suit, 1968.

WHAT DO THEY WANT

Sometimes he was just unsure. He was constantly reaching. I know along the years, in the music, he was always, always at the brink of, "What do they want? What are the demands?" Because, as the audience grew bigger, he didn't know what it was that they wanted. What to do to please them? It was too much, more often than not. Fans of any rock group, when they pay to go see a concert, they want to hear what they've already purchased on record. And Jim was trying to let them know that he'd gone past that. What he really wanted was to put his new message out, the new works, the new poetry. It was a message more than music.

He really was reaching out there. Because, it was a period of time when it wasn't just entertainment. It was a turn on. It was a period of

unrest, and political changes...and at times he held himself as the catalyst. And then he would turn around and say that *they* were the catalyst, that the audience was what was churning him onto new thoughts and new directions.

PLANNED SPONTANEITY & CONTROLLED CHAOS

He would reach out and play with people. Not in a malicious, offensive manner. But it was just part of his toyish, boyish manner and humor. He loved planned spontaneity and controlled chaos. Juggle those around.

Violence wasn't really a lever of his. It wasn't really a tool of his. It was there, but even in different induced states of emotions and feelings, it was more or less something that he talked about, screamed about and reached at, but didn't really employ. It was more or less mischief, not really malicious mischief, but just prankish mischief.

Authority was what we were striking out against, or what he was striking out against, and authority was everything that made everything else real. It didn't make it right, it made everything else real.

BOYISHLY BASHFUL

I remember the first time that Morrison and Jagger met. The Doors were booked to do a concert at the Hollywood Bowl. We were across the street at the Alta Cienega, Jim and I. And the office called. They were in a state of panic, "Jagger's here. He's coming across the street." I said, "Jim, ah...Jagger's across the street. He's coming over." Jim said, "That's alright."

There was a knock on the door, a very faint knock. Tap! Tap! Tap! And Jim nodded and I opened the door. And he said, "Hello, I'm Mick." And I said, "You sure as fuck are." It was like WOOO, you could feel the energy.

And Mick came in.

For Jim, who had slept on rooftops and on floors of friends' apartments, the Alta Cienega was deluxe, but in truth it was an old and dingy motel on a busy street corner. Definitely low rent. What was Jagger's reaction?

Mick made himself comfortable. There was no problem with that at all. In fact, it was what it was expected to be because the motel was right across the street from The Doors' office. No, he didn't look around and say what's this poverty hole. No.

Mick wanted to know if Jim meditated before he went on stage and Jim looked at him with that little perplexed boyish look and he says, "Meditate?" as if he didn't even understand the spelling of it.

And he said, "No, that's left up to John and Robby."

Meditate...here's Jim putting on black...

They talked about dancing on stage. Because Jagger was embarrassed about his dancing. He said he couldn't dance at all. He said the

Newspaper advertisement for the Magic Musical Festival, Devonshire Meadows, California, July 1967 where The Doors performed (opposite).

one thing he couldn't do was dance. And he and Jim both mentioned that it was becoming increasingly more difficult to feel comfortable and to feel smooth on stage dancing because the larger the audiences got, the larger the working area was and the less they could relate to it. Everything had to be more exaggerated. If you fell, you really had to fall.

They scoffed at how everything was overblown. They grew up with the movie idols, with the cowboy idols and everything and then all of the sudden they were center stage. They were both kind of boyishly bashful about it, and yet in full command. And it was very evident that they had mutual respect for each other's talent.

OTIS

It was the Christmas concerts at Winterland, San Francisco, three nights starting December 26, 1967. Otis Redding was the headliner and The Doors were second on the bill. Jim idolized Otis. On the tenth of December, Otis was killed in a plane crash. The word came from Bill Graham's office, "What should we do?" They wanted to know whether to cancel the concert, or what.

Jim said that he wanted to do the concert as a tribute. And The Doors were moved up to headline act. I did a brand new black velvet shirt with two-tone grey cobras embroidered around the left sleeve. Only on the left sleeve, because that's closest to the heart, which goes back to the American Indian. The left hand is the direct line from the heart to the spirit.

He asked for roses and I said, "What?" And he said he wanted red roses, blood red, not romance red, but blood red. In his own manner, he was putting out, laying out his tribute to Otis.

And that was also the night that the city's most famous drug maker was there with a new batch of acid. And he had laced everybody in the auditorium with acid and he came up to Jim and handed him acid and STP and I intercepted it. I said, "We got a show to do." And later Bill Graham came up to me and said, "Jim on acid?" And I said, "No," and I showed him all the pills that I had intercepted.

So, Jim appears on stage with the two dozen long-stemmed red roses in his arm. Very incongruous, Morrison, the black thread of rock 'n' roll, standing front stage with two dozen red roses. And he walked right up to the edge of the stage. Once again, one of those ledges that he was defying, just to see how close he could get. And as the music started, he looked out and said, "Poor Otis, dead and gone/left me here to sing his song/ Pretty little girl with a red dress on/ Poor Otis dead and gone." And he spilled the red roses all over everybody and broke into "When The Music's Over."

LEDGES & EDGES

Why did Jim feel he had to take everything to excess?

He wanted to push anything to the limit. Just like when he was walking on the edge of the ledge. He wanted to see how far far was. You know, it's like climbing out on a limb of a tree. He'd know that if you go past the fulcrum, guess what? And he would just try to see what would happen without looking for the insurance policy of a limb being below him. But, he did have a charm there.

Walking along the lip of the stage, 1968.

OUT ON THE PERIMETER

Like Philip, January was an experienced traveler in the psychedelic skies. Jim could count on him to bring them back, no matter where the trip took them.

And as Jim would take drugs, or do drugs, and it wasn't any one drug that he was pursuing, he would dabble in things. More like a little boy playing with matches, when he was told not to.

I can honestly say that anytime we took drugs, he never went into it mad, or out of an argument. They weren't used as an escape ...they were used more as a research vehicle, looking for something new, something different.

I remember the time after we had the concert at The Hollywood Bowl *(July 5, 1968)* and then came back to the all night ongoing party at the office. So, um...then after that, I guess about five, six in the morning, we went across the street to the two rooms we had at the Alta Cienega. And Jim said, "Did you bring what I asked?" Because, he called me up in San Francisco and asked me to bring down some mescaline he knew that I could get.

We emptied seventeen caps of mescaline sulfide needle crystals in one pint of orange juice, and seventeen caps of mescaline sulfide needle crystals in the other. And he drank a pint, and I drank a pint. And we got loaded. In fact, three days later, we were still peaking.

So, here we are out on the perimeter. Dancing on the perimeter, loaded on this mescaline. And we're oozing in and out of this and that. And three days later, we're still peaking. And this friend of Jim comes by. And she decides to take us for a ride in this convertible. So, Jim and I get into this convertible and we're riding up Topanga Canyon. We can't enjoy the ride, because the two of us are wearing ourselves out holding onto the seat to keep from flying out though the top. And we get up to this friend of her's house, and all of a sudden I have to heave. And I heave and I puke pure blood. Bright red blood. But, from here to where you're sitting. And I start to freak. And Jim says, "It's alright. You just had too much blood in you."

Hmm...so that equated everything. And everything came back to normal. And we went back to the motel, and hung out for another two days. Now understand, this is five days after the concert and I'm still peaking on these things. And Jim's looking over to me. He'd sit there across the room, and we wouldn't say anything. Then all of a sudden, we're having these incredible conversations without any words. All of a sudden he'd look over to me and he'd go, "Uh hoo." And it'd remind me to breathe. And I'd look over at him and remind him to breathe. And each of us would thank the other, because breathing seemed like the last thing that was important to us.

After the fifth day, in the evening, I called a driver and had him come and take me to LAX, because I had to get back to San Francisco

Above: Dancing on stage. Opposite: In the dressing room after a show at the Berkeley Community Theater, November 1967.

to tend to the business. The electric door opened, I walked into the airport. And walked right around and came right back out the other door. I went right back to the motel. I couldn't hang.

POETRY

What most people need to know is that over and above and far beyond the bullshit and all the fun was that Jim was probably one of the most sensitive and intelligent people that I've ever known. Very, very intelligent. Extremely well read.

He was very thirsty for knowledge and he always had a book with him. And always had a notebook. And it wasn't writing poetry. He called it taking notes. His notes were his poetry. He would write down thoughts, words as he collected them.

One thing that Jim couldn't do and one of the things that frustrated him the most, was that he really wanted people to accept him as a poet. Well, when you're in a rock 'n' group, people don't accept you as a poet, even though the songs are all poetry. The audience, they don't hold you as a poet.

WHERE TO TURN

There were times that he'd call me and it was like...just, "Ahhhhhh." And I would say, "What's the matter? You tired?" He'd say, "No. I'm just worn out. And don't know what to do, where to go." And I'd say, "What do you mean, where to go?" And he'd say, "Well..." What he meant was where to turn, what direction.

Like the time he handed me these two stacks of loose-leaf papers. We were in a motel room, at the Alta Cienega. So he handed me these two stacks of pages, and pushed the wastebasket over by the bed. And he said, "Edit these." And I'd say, "What do you mean?" And he said, "The ones that you like, put over here. And the ones you don't like, put into the wastebasket."

Well, I put the ones that I liked over here, in two stacks. The ones that went together in this theme and the ones that went together in this theme. I liked both the stacks, and the others I put over in another stack.

And he came in and without even looking at what was there, he picked up that far stack and put a match to them and dropped them in the wastebasket. I said, "What are you doing?" And he said, "You didn't like these?" And I said, "No." And he said, "I didn't either." I said, "You don't even know what I didn't like." He said, "Yeah, but you know what I'm trying to say." At that point I realized, I guess I did.

Handbill for a performance at the Shrine Auditorium, Los Angeles, December 1967.

Unpredictable

He had absolutely no respect for authority and usually he would take unnecessary risks to provoke it.

*R*ich Linnell and Bill Siddons have been close friends since high school. By being the right age, in the right place, at the right time, they carved out roles for themselves in the booming business of rock 'n' roll; Bill as the manager of bands like The Doors, and Rich as a concert producer and artists' representative.

RICH: I was born and raised in Los Angeles, and went to school in San Diego where I was good friends with Robby Krieger's twin brother Ronny. This was early 1967, and Ronny…I think he'd left school a year earlier than I had, but we remained friends. We'd both kind of, I don't want to say flunked out, but school wasn't our thing. The draft however was very important at that time, so it was important to stay in school to maintain your 2S deferment.

It was a very exciting time, filled with hope, a good time to be nineteen years old. The whole hippie thing was coming into fruition, and Sunset Strip was quite the spot, so we'd go up there and hang out, and drive up and down, and try to meet girls. We never did. And Ronny kept trying me to get me to come and see his brother's band.

Eventually Ronny Krieger succeeded in persuading Rich to see a Doors show.

RICH: So finally Ronny and I went up to Jim and Pam's place in Laurel Canyon, which is still there right across the street from the market, and we were supposed to drive them to the show. The Doors were playing at Ciro's that night *(April 1967)* and I didn't know anything about the band yet.

*Above: Rich Linnel, 1969.
Opposite: Jim leaping during a song at the Westbury Music Fair, Connecticut, April 1968.*

As we were climbing the stairs, Ronny turns to me and he goes, "Be kind of quiet, be cool, he doesn't like a lot of noise." So I said, "Okay, that's no problem." We walk in and introductions were made, "Hi, this is Rich, this is Jim, this is Pam, hello, how do you do?" And those were the only words spoken for about twenty minutes while Pam and Jim got ready. And they got in the car, drove on down the hill, and again nothing was being said. I didn't want to say anything. I was the new guy in town, and I was taking Ronny's lead.

We dropped them off and they went in the back door, and we went in the front. We sat on the floor in front of the stage and about twenty minutes later the band comes out. And here's this guy who was previously just…quiet is an understatement, who suddenly just lurches into incredible histrionics on stage. Screaming and yelling and rolling around, and I was just going, "What?" And from that moment, I was hooked, I was a big fan.

After a while Ronny and Rich started carrying and setting up The Doors' sound equipment, because as Rich says, "They had nobody else to do it."

We weren't particularly hardworking in that regard, but we would have a good time, and we'd get to meet girls and that kind of stuff.

A few months later we had a trip planned to San Francisco, so I called my good friend Bill Siddons and I said, "Bill, do you wanna go up to San Francisco with us. We got to carry The Doors' equipment." So he did.

SCARED TO DEATH

BILL: I grew up in the San Gabriel Valley, a more or less low income area. And in my teen years moved to Hermosa Beach. From the time I moved, I surfed regularly. And it was my best friend Rich Linnell who taught me how to really surf. We met on a bus going to a high school swim meet and by the time we got back from the meet we

Bill Siddons assumes a problem-solving stance, 1970.

were best friends and it's been that way ever since.

I graduated from high school in 1965 and then went to Cal State Long Beach. After Rich started helping with The Doors' equipment, he started telling me about them but I wasn't very interested. I didn't know who The Doors were, 'cause they hadn't had a hit yet. When he offered me a trip to San Francisco, I said, "OK, I'll go."

Flying to a concert, August 1968.

We ended up sitting in the audience at this show at the Avalon Ballroom *(May 12, 1967)*, watching this maniac. What I remember is Jim on stage. I wasn't affected one way or the other by meeting him, but when I saw him on stage I was more emotionally gripped and moved and disturbed than I had ever been at any similar type of thing.

I remember thinking, WHAT? What is he saying? What is he doing? I don't get it. And then he said something about, "Awkward instant/And the first animal is jettisoned,/Legs furiously pumping/ Their stiff green gallop" *(from Jim's poem "Horse Latitudes")* and I went, "This guy is completely out of his mind." But I was moved by it, I could feel it. It was the first time poetry had been a movie to me, the images were so strong that they came to mind in photo form. I could see the horses jumping off the boat, I could see them drowning.

So what was my first impression of Jim? He scared me to death.

CONTROLLING THEIR OWN DESTINY

BILL: At that San Francisco concert, when Robby saw me coming up the stairs with an amp in each hand and behind me Rich and Ronny on either side of one amp, that was easy math for him: that's four times as efficient, hire that kid.

So I traveled around the country working with The Doors that summer of 1967. "Light My Fire" was released in April 1967 and by the time I started working with them in May the record was starting to happen. I was eighteen, nineteen years old. I didn't go to meetings. I couldn't hang out in the bar because I was too young. But I was raised with a very strong work ethic and a commitment to do what I promised. Whatever I said I could do, I did.

By mid-January 1968, The Doors bought back their contract from the two Los Angeles men who were managing them. Robby asked Bill, "How would you like to be our manager?" Bill replied, "What's a manager do?" Robby said, "Well, just answer the phones and we'll have meetings and decide what to do."

Why did a band with a number one single and a million unit selling album hire a nineteen-year-old college surfer to be their personal manager?

BILL: It was absolutely stupid to hire me. I had no idea what I was doing. They, on the other hand, were controlling their own destiny. They had discovered early in their career that a lot of people had a very different set of motives than theirs.

RICH: We were in Phoenix, Arizona and it was February 1968 and there was a bomb scare so everybody had to evacuate the building. So we had to hang out for forty-five minutes. So Jim started asking me questions, "Now, Rich, what do you do? You know, I see you around a lot, what do you do?" This was just after I'd produced my first concert, and this was the second concert I'd produced, so I said "Well, I'm producing these shows." And he goes, "What do you mean, 'producing the shows'?" "Well, you rent the hall and you get all the equipment together

Left: Cops in uniform patrolled the halls and auditoriums of most Doors concerts.
Opposite: At the Fillmore East, New York City, September 9, 1967.

and you do the advertising and sell the tickets, and if enough people come you make money, and if they don't, you lose money." He kind of gets this look on his face and he goes, "Oh, you mean you do this?"

So we talked for awhile, and Jim was very impressed with the fact that someone my age was able to do this and he said, "You mean we can just do this ourselves? We don't need to use all these other people? No one needs to tell us what to do here?" And I go, "Yeah, that's right." He says, "Oh, this is great, I like this."

He was impressed with the fact that we could control our own destiny. That was important to him. And it was important that he had people around him that would help him facilitate controlling his own destiny. The fact that I was doing one thing, Bill Siddons was doing something else, and we were younger than he was, was something that was…he liked that idea.

RESISTING AUTHORITY

BILL: One of the things that made him real interesting was that Jim always did what he wanted, not what other people wanted. So he would just choose not to go along so that he could set his own course. He did it by virtue of will.

One of Jim's real strengths was that he could see through any of us, whatever game we were trying to play, he could see behind that. He could read anybody he was talking to.

Jim seemed to resist authority in any form it took, but if Bill was to do his job, he would at times have to dictate to Jim what needed to be done.

BILL: Personally he could dominate me anytime he needed to dominate me. But he knew I came to him with what reality was. I couldn't make him do anything, but he would respond to me because he knew I was telling him the truth. He was kinda charmed by that, "I don't want to embarrass the kid." So he'd go along with it.

So as an authority figure, yeah, but not as a father figure, he was always the father, I was the son who knew better. That's how it worked.

And Jim kept reminding me all the time that just because these were the rules doesn't mean it's OK. From the New Haven incident to any of those professional problems we had, Jim was the one who made me aware of why they were happening. What the conflict really was. Who was coming after him, how he was threatening them. Without him, I'd a missed a lot of that stuff. I sort of did anyway. He knew what was going to happen, I didn't see what was happening. I was too busy doing my job.

Opposite: The day before a court appearance in Phoenix, Arizona in 1969, Jim's attorney, Max Fink, took him to an expensive men's shop for a complete sartorial makeover. Jim never again wore the outfit.

Jim provokes the audience as the concert promoter attempts to free his leg from a fan's grasp in Cleveland, July 1968.

PROVOKE AND CHALLENGE

The times were changing rapidly and radically for young people on the West Coast in 1967. In step with the student protesters, the new bands were setting the tempo for the change. Because they appeared to be initiators of the swelling youth revolution, the rock bands were often on the front lines of the clash with the established order.

BILL: First of all, Jim was willing to suffer in his pursuit of the truth. I saw him a number of times in his life do things that were absolutely threatening to his personal health.

He provoked people that he knew could fuck with him. He would confront a policeman and engage him in verbal warfare till the point where the guy had to hit him with a club to shut him up. He was fearless in a lot of ways. He didn't have the same kind regard for his own well-being. He had absolutely no respect for authority and usually he would take unnecessary risks to provoke it.

In retrospect I look at Jim as a guy that had the curse of challenge. He had to always challenge. I mean for example walking through customs in Toronto, Canada. We had been through a couple of customs

before together. And the customs guys had been very officious, asking dumb questions and just making you feel like, "Yes, sir. No, sir. Yes, sir. No, sir." Jim got down on his hands and knees and started barking at these guys. And I'm going, "How am I going to get this guy through customs if he's barking." But he had to make that statement: you guys are treating us like dogs so I'm going to bark at you. Of course not many people got the statement, I don't even think I got it, except by growing up a little bit and looking back at why he did what he did.

RIOT

Being on stage offered Jim opportunities to use his will on a large group of people to see what sort of change he could produce. How he would do it on any particular night no one knew, not even Jim.

RICH: To distill it to one word: unpredictable. You never quite knew what he was going to do, which was half of the excitement of a Doors concert. However, the down side is that you can't be unpredictable indefinitely. Initially, I can remember, I wondered, "What's he going to do on stage next?" Some nights he would just stand and sing into the

At one point during the Cleveland concert, Jim jumped from the stage into the audience and was swallowed up by fans. Jim's hand is visible on the microphone.

microphone, and other nights he would go wild. A lot of it had to do with what he felt at that moment. Sometimes he felt like letting loose and sometimes he didn't. It was exciting because there was always an edge, there was always an element of anticipation.

I think Jim liked a crowd to be near him. When we could, we would do no chairs on the floor of the auditorium or hall, so the crowd could get closer to the stage and kind of hang around the stage. He would talk to them and he talked to them as equals more than talking down to them.

It got him in a lot of trouble in Phoenix because it was right after Richard Nixon was elected in 1968, and Jim wasn't thrilled, so he started to give a little talk about, "We're not gonna take four more years of this crap, are we? We've had enough of it!" Of course the audience responded and moved closer to the stage, the police freaked out, and Jim kept taunting the crowd and the police. And next day in the paper were the headlines, "Riot at the Coliseum." Now, by no stretch of the imagination was it a riot, a few people got jostled, one cop got his hat flipped off his head, and probably a few people fell over. But that was their perception in Arizona: it was a riot. And of course they blamed Jim for it.

EXPERIMENTING

There are lots of stories about Jim's wild ways in those early days just as the band was beginning to gain national recognition.

BILL: Well, this is where you have a lot of trouble separating myth from reality. I joined up with them at the end of the acid days and in the early months of the alcohol days, and Jim didn't have any other real drug problems that I ever saw. He never took pills, or did barbiturates or anything else.

One weekend, in 1967, we played the Action House on Long Island. In the afternoon, while I was setting up the equipment, Jim drank at the bar and by the time he walked on stage he was completely incoherent. After it was over, I went up to the bartender and said, "He ran a tab here, I need to know how much he drank, can you look up the tab?" The guy counted up the drinks and said, "Twenty-six shots of VO Canadian whiskey." I knew twenty-six shots was enough to go to the hospital for, and he drank it in two or three hours.

All I remember him saying is, "I wanted to find out what would happen." But he knew what would happen, didn't he?

I don't think he reflected on it before he did it. I think he reflected on it afterward. I think escape was a big part of it, I think experimentation was a big part of it, and I think just pushing everybody else's buttons was a part of it. Like, "How fucked up can I get and get away with it? How much will they put up with?" He often did things that tested how much people would put up with.

When his hair got too long, Jim would cut it himself. His method was to gather in one hand all the hair that fell below his shoulder and cut it straight across with a scissor. Compare the photo above with the one opposite that was taken several hours later.

RICH: Sometimes it was hard to tell if he was drunk. And even drunk, he was lucid, which always kind of amazed me. I'm sure he drank a lot more than I did, but I never witnessed him throwing drinks or glasses around or becoming an obnoxious drunk.

At first it seemed to all be in good fun. We were all experimenting with alcohol, or with drugs more than alcohol. It was a time to experiment. And Jim's indulgences seemed to me always to be more something of trying it on rather than being possessed by it. Although with alcohol after awhile, it became apparent there was a problem. Drinking seemed to be his sole vice. I couldn't tell you, "The guy's an alcoholic." I don't think that crossed my mind with that clarity of thought. But, it was clear that drinking was a problem.

There was little social awareness of alcoholism in the mid-sixties as a progressive disease. All of Jim's friends were drinking, and none of us knew enough to convince to him that he needed to get off booze and into a recovery program.

BILL: I knew he had a lot of serious problems. I didn't know what they were. I just knew that he would put more alcohol into his body than anybody....I thought he was trying to commit suicide, because the quantities didn't make any sense to me. He operated in Jimland, and nobody lived there but him.

ASSOCIATES
As a legal partnership, The Doors' internal agreement specified that the members had to act in concert, everyone agreeing before any venture was undertaken or important decision made.

RICH: At the beginning, for me being late '66, early '67, Jim always seemed to be a little bit apart from the band. As time went on, Jim became more and more distant from the band. He would arrive differently, he'd come by himself, he'd leave earlier or later.

Jim would have his little group in the dressing room and the three guys would have theirs. Robby, as recently as a few years ago would say, "Yeah, for a long time it was the three of us against Jim. And then when we didn't have Jim to go after anymore, then we fought amongst ourselves."

In 1968 the Buick Division of General Motors approached The Doors with an offer to buy the rights to their song, "Light My Fire," for an ad campaign.

BILL: One of the few times I saw Jim angry was when he found out about, "Come on Buick, Light My Fire." Out of control. He felt betrayed. His partners had betrayed him, they had sold out to corporate America without asking him.

I was there when he told them, "How could you do this to me? This is my band, too. How could you make that decision without me?"

One of them said, "Well, man, you didn't tell us where you were going, and the offer would have expired."

"So what?" He just didn't get it. Whether he was gone for a day or a month, it didn't matter, but you don't sell out to the establishment. Postpone it or cancel but don't give my soul away.

That was the end of the dream. That was the end of that era of Jim's relationship with the other members of the band; from then on it was business. That was the day Jim said, "I don't have partners anymore, I have associates."

Another band might have dissolved, but The Doors endured. Jim reached beyond rock to pursue other areas of creativity: poetry, film, screenplays, and he waited, sometimes not very patiently, for his freedom from the obligations and promises that tied him to the other members of the band.

A NEW PERSON

RICH: You know, he'd gone over there *(to Paris in the spring of 1971)* to be kind of obscure and to be a poet, and he hadn't been there but three or four months I guess, and it seemed to me that he just never had a chance to really stretch his wings in his new life. And I think I was as saddened as much by that as I am anything. Cause I knew he wanted to be another person, be a new person. And it just seemed to me that he never really had the opportunity to do that, to fulfill that wish. And that was sad.

Left: Jim was not pleased when he learned that Buick had purchased the rights to use "Light My Fire" in an ad campaign. Following: The Doors at the taping of "Critique", a PBS TV show, New York City, 1968.

On the Very Edge

You could take away anything you wanted from Jim Morrison, but don't mess with his freedom.

R on Allan and I knew each other only slightly in the sixties. He remembered me from the time I was editing a documentary film about The Doors, Feast of Friends. Recently, we spent a long afternoon talking about everything, swapping stories and reminiscing. Ron's understanding, openness, and humanity inform everything he says. A musician and songwriter himself, Ron could appreciate Jim's talents in those areas. Playing in clubs on the Sunset Strip, living in the Hollywood hills, hanging out with musicians, dancers, artists, and an assorted mix of crazies, Ron had a ringside table at the nation's best sideshow, "Hollywood Meets the Psychedelic Revolution."

Above: Ron Allan, 1968. Opposite: Something or someone amuses Jim at the Felt Forum, New York City, January 1970.

I come from San Antonio, Texas. I lived in West Los Angeles from my teenage years on and started putting bands together in '63 and so I was going up to Hollywood, up to the Strip and playing in all the clubs and stuff. Writing songs.

I was playing at the London Fog with the Magic Tramps and at the time we were just a trio, and the Fog was a place that you could work material out. The owner, Jesse James, would pay twenty bucks a night for the band and let you have a couple of drinks. There was never much of a crowd in there, so you could just kind of work your songs out and play. The Doors came in a few months later. (*The Doors played the London Fog during March, April, and May 1966.*) They were great from the very beginning.

Jim was good, he was good, he went for it and that's what was important. You didn't look at him and say, "There's a guy that's doubting his abilities." This was a guy that had questionable abilities with no doubt at all. I mean he was just doing it. I thought, "Here is guy that has called himself a singer and he believes it and thus he is a singer." Boy, he committed to the song. He'd just get into it.

He looked really bad. He'd been sleeping who knows where in the same clothes for three or four days and then he'd climb on stage and he'd look very thin and kind of pale and very wrinkled up, but the vitality that he had coming out of this crumpled being was amazing, I mean that was just amazing. And he was drinking and…the London Fog had a stage that was six or seven feet off the ground, quite a ways up, and it was very small, very, very small, hardly enough room for the instruments, so Jim had just a little area in front, you know a couple of feet space, but he would choose to sing on the very edge of the stage, hang his toes over and sing and there was a cement floor below him. You always thought, "Man, this guy's going to fall off of this thing."

When we first started hanging together, it wasn't over musical interests at all. It just seemed we all related the same way. And then later he started…well, we had a piano downstairs at the little rehearsal area we had and we'd go down there and we wrote some stuff together, you know, me and him and Freddy. And then we started getting musically together on things.

It seems to me all of that stuff we wrote down there was just stuff that just started flowing. I'd start playing and he'd start singing and then start writing things down. It all seemed to just come from the spur of the moment.

He would start putting things together, and he'd scratch 'em down on pieces of paper and stuff. I don't know what happened to a lot of it. I know some was just left behind and swept into the trash can, it was no big deal, we were just writing all the time and having a good time.

I mean it was just guys drinking and sittin' around a piano and having a good time.

THE STRIP IN THE SIXTIES

The Sunset area of Hollywood was such a close family in those early days that everybody knew everybody else, and everybody was tripping. Everybody was on acid, so I mean, you're taking acid with people sitting at the next table, you're getting to know them, you know it was a big family up there at the time.

There was a lot of LSD on the streets and LSD in the early days was legal, where pot was a felony. So if you got caught with a joint, you could

Backstage after a performance at the Kaleidoscope on Sunset Boulevard, March 1968. Jim sips wine as a friend mops his brow.

do a year if they wanted to be nasty about it. And you could take acid legally. So you'd find guys all up and down the street with containers of acid you could go buy for a couple of bucks, so everybody was lit up on the street. It was a great place to go because of the music, there were great musicians in all the clubs and the streets themselves were alive. Here was this very colorful, open, wonderful music and everything else going on, plus everything that everyone saw when we were tripping. It just opened the whole world up to you. Even the stoplights looked terrific, the glow of the lights and everything. A lot of acid. A lot of music.

It was a revolution. It was a peaceful revolution. I mean, what did people preach? They preached "Love." It wasn't an angry thing because when you take LSD and your mind is open, you become very soulful.

GRAVEYARD POEM

It was a night we had played a club called the Sea Witch *(late '67 or early '68)* which was on Sunset Strip, right across from Ben Franks. And we had been hanging for about three days and were very wasted by the time the gig started and I was playing about a half hour into the set and I passed out on stage, fell off the organ and passed out, and Freddy the singer came up and started playing keyboards and Jim got up and started singing. I was out for a couple hours, I guess, and then after that gig we went over to a couple girls' house that we knew, a couple girls that hung with our band, and we went over there and we were pretty drunk and we took some acid and we saw the graveyard across the street, right there on Gower. Gower, just south of Santa Monica Boulevard. A very large graveyard. And it was like, what?, two or three in the morning and we were looking at that graveyard and we figured, that'd be a real good place to go right now. So me and Freddy and Jim, and the two girls, climbed the walls there and went into the graveyard. The minute we got into the graveyard, we saw a white rabbit and we chased the rabbit and it got away and we just stayed in there and walked around. It was like almost defying death in a way, to embrace it.

Peggy, one of the girls, got freaked out by the whole thing, she lay down on a grave and started crying and kicking her feet and really screaming and crying and stuff.

> We scaled the wall
> We tripped thru the graveyard
> Ancient shapes were all around us
> No music but the wet grass
> felt fresh beside the fog
>
> Two made love in a silent spot
> one chased a rabbit into the dark
> A girl got drunk & made the dead
> And I gave empty sermons to my head
>
> Cemetery cool & quiet
> Hate to leave
> your sacred lay
> Dread the milky coming of the day

(from Wilderness)

And we went back in there a number of times after that, late at night. "Well, what should we do?" "Let's go in the graveyard." And we'd go back in there. That had to be around February 1968.

Jim would be bearded one day and clean-shaven the next. Then, after a few weeks, he'd start to grow a beard again.

BAR FIGHTS

Jim and Ron and Freddy hit the bars and nightclubs more than a few nights a week. And it was during this time when Jim's reputation as a barroom brawler was established.

I think that things have a way of going from one ear to the next to the next. We fought a lot, me and Jim, but we fought in fun, just like kids will wrestle, you'd be walking around and you'd grab your buddy and start wrestling and then you laugh it off in the end and you go and do something else. And we did a lot of that and, because he hung out in bars, and because it had been out that he fights, even though the fights were friendly, all of a sudden these two things kind of come together: fights and bars equals bar fights.

But, no, he would never look for trouble and if it came to him, he was intelligent enough and likeable enough to be able to say one or two words and smooth it over just like that. I never saw him even have to do that, though. So, I just can't imagine bar fights.

I never saw him angry, I never saw him lose his temper. I don't even know if he was capable of that. I just never saw it. He wasn't one to fight against things. If something came up, it was just like, "Yeah, oh well." And that's all he would give it.

GOING TO THE MOON

There was never any morphine or heroin or anything like that. But the thing with Jim that was amazing, and I saw this happen more than once, we'd be over at some girl's house or whatever, wherever, and somebody would walk up, I don't mean just somebody off the streets, somebody in the house who knew us would walk up with a handful of pills, like three, four, five pills and not explain what they were or anything and they'd just go up to Jim and he'd open his mouth, they'd pour them in and he'd chase them down.

Didn't know what trip he was going on, had no idea what he was going to be experiencing in the next few hours. He didn't know if it was acid, speed, or what. It was just the adventure. The balls of that. Can you imagine the nerve of doing that and not even knowing what experience you're going to be having now. Man, you're going to the moon in a few minutes. It was that I'm going someplace new, so let's get on with it. It was that type of adventure and willingness to experience and experiment. And just see what else he could see.

Jim was into alcohol and not drugs, though, I mean he was not into drugs. He liked taking acid and that was to travel with and make his brain see more and it wasn't just to get screwed up on. He was not on any kind of drug consistently of any kind. Even pot he didn't care smoking that much, every once in awhile he'd have a hit but...he wasn't big on that. He liked drinking.

Drinking and eating at the Lucky-U.

anything, ever, he wasn't afraid of anything, he had no fear, but this thing of putting him in jail, that was the first time I saw anything at all that was like, "Oh man, this is not good."

But everything was on a decline anyway, and the police were getting heavier and heavier on the Strip. The strip in '69 was nothing like it was in '67. It just kind of deteriorated.

It ended, this brief springtime of bright colors and music, in 1968 when in the space of a few months Robert Kennedy and Rev. Martin Luther King were assassinated and the demonstrators and working press at the Democratic National Convention in Chicago were brutally suppressed by the police. In November Richard Nixon was elected president. The nation, long in the grip of a draining and divisive war in Viet Nam, was sunk in gloom. The Summer of Love, celebrated with such enthusiasm in 1967, was dissolving like a dream, and we would be walking into a new harsher world in 1969.

On March 1, 1969 Jim performed in Miami. Later in the year, Charles Manson and his band of hippie commune crazies went on a drug-induced spree, killing Sharon Tate and six others to put an end to flower power and the belief in the salvation of LSD. And at Altamont on December 6, the Hells Angels overturned our belief in the saving grace of rock 'n' roll. No more would we be able to see music as a way to bring people together. Very surely we knew that the violence was always there waiting. Now, Peace and Love, those twin symbols of the hippie and war protest movements, were worthless tokens. It was over and the only thing that kept it going was a little leftover forward momentum, and commercialization of the symbols of the dream: the packaging of the Love Generation.

Anyone with both feet on the ground made sure that their passport was current.

CHANGE IT

Near the end of our conversation we were talking about Jim going to Paris and what that meant and suddenly a question popped into my head. "What do you think Jim wanted to do besides what he was doing?"

Change it. He wanted to change it, that's why he left. He wanted change, it was just, how do you do that. And how do you do that, especially when you're Jim Morrison? He just was fed up with the superstar, sex idol that he was expected to be, or the drunken guy he was expected to be. I think he would have liked to do movies. I think that would have been a natural progression for him. More poetry, of course, always more poetry.

Just get out in a different world, a different world for him than what he'd been used to over those last years. But, you go somewhere else and things aren't always the way you'd imagine they might be, and you're still in the same spot, even though you've changed locations. I think he just would have liked to lead a normal life for a little bit, I think that would have been a wonderful vacation for him.

Red Lights

Before I knew him I misunderstood his demeanor, his walk, his kind of lackadaisical or lazy or laconic persona as being arrogant. At least arrogant.

Ginny Ganahl started working in The Doors office at 8512 Santa Monica Boulevard in November 1968 when she was twenty years old. She would stay long enough to get the office humming smoothly and help Jim with the first of his self-published works.

I had never been a fan of The Doors. I was really into the Buffalo Springfield. And I liked The Byrds. I thought Jim Morrison was such a phony when I'd see him on TV or see him around town. He seemed like he was just trying so hard to either act cool, or act stoned, which people did. People actually tried to act stoned.

And so it was amazing to me when I did meet him. And I met him like probably the first or second day when I started work at the office. It was just amazing to me to find that he was so gentle and genuine.

He wanted to know about me. You know he had that way of just bringing out the best in people. He really was kind of drawing me out. I felt like he was interested at least to an extent in who I was. And he was so relaxed. I don't think I've met anybody in my whole life who was so truly cool in almost every situation I ever saw him in. And I was struck with that the first day.

And I just was real impressed with his gentleness and his lack of pretense. I had always misunderstood what he was about. I'd always thought he was so pretentious.

Before I knew him I misunderstood his demeanor, his walk, his kind of lackadaisical or lazy or laconic persona as being arrogant. At least arrogant. And I really thought that he was trying to act cool. Like he'd seen James Dean maybe. Kind of drag around slowly. You know, that kind of vacant look or something. I felt like he was pretending. But

Above: Ginny at work in The Doors office, 1969. Opposite: In Mexico City, Jim stands in front of a mural by Juan O'Gorman.

when I met him and then ever after, whenever I saw him in the office or wherever, I knew that wasn't so; I knew that he just really was like that. He was that laid back. It wasn't that he was trying to act cool or trying to look cool. It was that he was cool.

And then when I saw him at The Forum, in December of '68 I was totally blown away by the way he handled that crowd. I had just really never seen anything like it. And of course he was such a tremendous singer too. I had never really given him much credit for that, either.

ODDS WERE

You know what he was like in the car. If he was driving on Santa Monica or down La Cienega, he might sort of sideswipe a car and then kind of change lanes erratically. And then you know, hit another car. And when the car finally stops, for whatever reason, he'd get out and walk away. And whatever he'd been wearing for the day or two, or three previous, if it was old or smelly, he would put it in the trunk and walk away from that too.

You know how we used to cross the street from the office to go to the Phone Booth. (*The Phone Booth was Jim conveniently close to The Doors' office.*) It was a very wide intersection with the railroad tracks running down the center. Jim would wait until the light turned red. He just would. He just had to. And then he would play this very sort of laconic, rubber leg matador with the cars. I mean it was just nutsy. But, you couldn't do anything about it. I crossed that street with him enough to know that's what he was going to do.

So, you'd go ahead and cross the street. And go in the bar and get a booth, and sit and wait. You knew, odds were, he'd make it. He just had that thing about it. He had that kind of…whether it was contrariness or a real deep-seated rebellion or whether it was just fun, or a challenge, or whatever. He just had this thing about driving and walking through traffic, where he had to make it more dangerous than it already was.

Ginny's story reminded me of the many times I crossed that same street with Jim. He would either wait until the light

Having fun in Seattle, 1970.

turned red and then run across in front of the oncoming cars, or he'd run across when the traffic was the heaviest and get a great kick out of dodging death or injury. It wasn't a competitive game; he didn't expect, or even want, you to do the same thing. For Jim it made an ordinary action, like crossing the street, just a little bit more fun. "Whew," he'd say once he made it safely to the other side, "That was close," as if the cars and drivers he had confronted were aiming for him. And then we'd laugh about it, still buzzing with the thrill.

ODE

The Doors were scheduled to played The Aquarius Theater in Los Angeles on July 21, 1969 and Jim was determined to make the evening memorable. On July 3, 1969 word came from England that Brian Jones, the founding and most outrageous member of the Rolling Stones, had drowned in the swimming pool of his home.

I remember the day. I remember that I heard about Brian Jones' death on the radio on the way to work that morning.

Jim called that morning, and I don't know who might have brought it up first, but somebody said, "Geez, it's a drag about Brian Jones." And he said he'd written a poem. As I recall, he said, "Do you want to hear it?" And I said, "Yes, of course." And he read it. And I was mesmerized.

The poem that Jim had composed in the first few hours after Brian Jones' tragic and unexpected death was entitled, "Ode to LA while Thinking of Brian Jones, Deceased." The poem concludes with these lines:

Will he Stink
Carried heavenward
Thru the halls
of music

No chance.

Requiem for a heavy
That smile
That porky satyr's
leer
has leaped upward

into the loam

I doubt if I said anything about being moved by it, but I was really impressed with the poem. I had heard a lot and read a lot of Jim's poetry and lyrics, but I was very moved by that poem. I thought it was brilliant. And the end, "That smile/That porky satyr's/ leer/ has leaped upward/ into the loam," was just so Jim Morrison to me. And yet it was Brian Jones too. I honestly felt like he really, really captured something. And I don't know what I might have said to encourage him to get it printed. But the Aquarius date was close enough so that he could print it and pass it out as a tribute.

Ginny helped Jim prepare the manuscripts of his first two books of writings.

He was 100% sure about those two books, *The Lords* and *The New Creatures.* And I remember when it was all done, and they came, and he had the books. And he had signed mine. And we had made some decisions on who was going to get what and everything, he was so pleased. He said, "Now I can die happy."

I mean, he said it pretty lightheartedly. But it meant that much to him, even though they were self-published. He was an artist and it was a limited edition of his work.

Opposite: On stage, Asbury Park, New Jersey, 1968.

TEASE

I was very young. And he loved to tease me. He loved to embarrass me. I think that…I still blush once in a while. But, in those days it was not that difficult to make me blush. And he just loved to do it. And he was just going to do whatever he could to make me die of embarrassment. So, in that way he was like an older brother who got off on teasing me.

During the course of the nine months that I worked there in that little office and saw Jim, I would say that 98% of the time Jim was a gentleman, a real gentle person. And carried himself as a poet, as a real working poet.

I never saw him be mean. I never saw him be cruel to anybody, and he never raised his voice in anger to anyone. It was like he had an understanding, I think. A bigger understanding than any of us had at the time about the flow of things. The inevitability of things. And he was really capable of just sitting back and being an observer to a great extent. He loved being an observer of situations. So a lot of the time he wasn't making anything happen. And he wasn't even commenting. He would just sit and watch.

I'm constantly amazed, even now, or even more now because of how much time we've had to live without him and think about him and all, how mature he was for someone who, after all, died so young. I just think in some way he had his act and his whole life, not just his professional life, together.

Snakeskin Jacket

Jim reached over with a bottle and broke it over Babe's head. I said, "Jim, that was a really rotten thing to do," and he said, "Oh Yeah?"

Michael McClure was there early, in New York and San Francisco, during those struggling, beginning mid-fifties years that marked the renaissance of American poetry. Besides being a playwright, novelist, teacher, and activist, he is one of just a handful of truly original American poets of this century.

He speaks with the quick authority of someone who knows what he's talking about, and his idiom is all his own: part prairie, part urban hipster, part San Francisco seer. Alternating between excitement and thoughtfulness, the rhythm and cadence of his voice swing his sentences in wider and wider arcs. The way his observations and reflections flowed back toward uncovering the deepest wellspring within his memory made me think he was interviewing himself about our mutual friend.

Jim had confidence in his own ability, and sought validation by someone whose work he admired; a writer whose judgement he could trust. In Michael, Jim found both a mentor and a friend.

Michael Hamilburg was going with Pam's sister Judy, and Jim wanted to meet me, and he heard that Michael was my agent. Actually Hamilburg later became Jim's literary agent. So Hamilburg got a hold of me while I was in New York at rehersals of my play *The Beard*, and arranged for us to meet at a bar in the Village. Jim had on leather pants, as a matter of fact, I had on leather pants too. And it was one of those things where we walked into the bar, Hamilburg introduced us, I sat down and took one look at Jim, he took one look at me and we decided we didn't like each other. And you know how young men are. We sat and glared, sort of cold fish eyeballing each other out of existence. I don't remember how it happened, but anyway one of us bought the

Above: Michael McClure, 1967. Opposite: Jim sometimes wore charms given to him by others. After a few hours or days, he would give them to someone else, or leave them behind in a motel room. Possessions never stuck to him very long.

other one a drink and we started talking, and we fell in. It took us a few chilling minutes to get there and Michael Hamilburg told me that he remembers getting a cold stomach about it. He moved away, it was too much; he went down to the other end of the bar.

The initial wariness changed pretty quickly into a warm response to one another. I liked Jim's intelligence, I liked his style, I liked the way his mind moved, and I liked the way he moved. Pretty well integrated human being, both physically adept and mentally adept, and the whole individual working in one direction. You could sense the poet there.

STATE OF CRISIS

The role of a poet in society today is the same role as that of any artist and that is to maintain the thoroughfares, to maintain these pathways of the imagination in a society that would close down the pathways of the imagination. In other words, to keep the imagination moving. I mean all of the arts have the same function, and all of them are to maintain a kind of state of crisis, to keep a state of crisis in existence, a state where we're alive and not just robots filling out social positions one after another.

Would Jim have agreed?

Yeah I think Jim would have agreed, Jim would have agreed with that wholeheartedly.

A BABY KEROUAC

What prompted him to start writing poems would be that he was responding to poems that he saw or heard, poems that spoke to him.

You see the possibilities of the play of imagination within an art form and then that art form begins to speak to you and then you wish to perform such feats yourself. For instance, you listen to blues and you decide you're going to sing blues. You say, "Oh my god, Muddy Waters is sensational." Listening to the complexity of that form, how might I do something like this?

The beginning of poetry writing is in a response to poetry. A baby kitten starts chasing mice 'cause it's going to be a cat; a baby eagle starts to fly, practicing standing on the edge of its nest, beating its wings; a baby Kerouac starts typing a novel.

Jim had a lyric gift, I mean a lyric gift not in the sense of song lyric, but poetry. Jim had a gift for poetry and then he also discovered he could sing and he could write songs, and he did the smart thing: he kept them separate and the more separate he kept them the better off he was.

A 1970 poster announcing a poetry reading.

THE PORT HOLE

Jim could not do anything halfway. If he drank, he had to finish the bottle. When he took LSD he did it every day in ever-increasing amounts. When he performed, he would have played until he dropped with exhaustion if local regulations didn't impose a curfew. It was excess for the sake of experience, the raw material of a poet's art. The road of excess may lead, as William Blake wrote, to the palace of wisdom, but it can also destroy the traveler in the process.

Jim was fascinated with Rimbaud's idea of the arranged derangement of the senses. When you arrange to derange the normal balance of your senses, whether you do it with alcohol, or lack of sleep, or with starvation, or whether you do it with sex, or whether you do it with drugs, you not only add to the body of your knowledge but you jar the body of knowledge so that you are looking out in a different way. And once you look out in a different way, you widen the field. It's as if you made the porthole that looks out into the world a trifle larger, and this is what a young poet really must do, what a meaningful young poet must do —a young poet writing about acts of adventure and consciousness and perception.

NILE INSECT EYES

In *The Lords: Notes on Vision,* Jim alchemically deconstructed his own UCLA film school thesis into this incredible document. I think the book is a deconstruction and compression and compaction of a longer document, which is a very good way for a poet to work. It's profound for a young man to have and put together that many insights. Some of the insights might not be original, but the assemblage of them together creates a very unique, philosophical work. He shows an incredible capacity for dealing with information, both inventive information and real information. It's a strong work.

Jim's book *The New Creatures* is a book of imagistic poetry with hints of the seventeenth century, with hints of Elizabethan theater, and with hints of classical mythology, and it has a romantic personal viewpoint. I use romantic in a nineteenth century Shelleyian/Keatsian sense: "Snakeskin jacket/Indian eyes...

> Snakeskin jacket
> Indian eyes
> Brilliant hair
>
> He moves in disturbed
> Nile Insect
> Air
>
> (from *The New Creatures*)

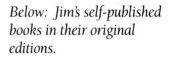

Below: Jim's self-published books in their original editions.

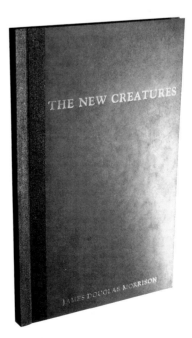

I mean, this is a nineteenth century poem, very personal, yet the poetry itself is adeptly twentieth century imagist poetry. It's almost mainstream, and it's good poetry, real fine poetry. It's as good as anybody in his generation; there's no better poet in Jim's generation.

This is as good an autobiographical poem, as good a short autobiographical poem, as I know, especially considering its compression. Here we have a poem of what, six imagistic lines. I mean one thinks of a sonnet of Shelley. It's like a flake, an obsidian chip flaked out of a sonnet of Shelley's. One can also think of rock songs, at the same time, I mean, think of how simple-minded and yet beautiful…

THE ADEPT

Jim asked me to come over to London to talk to Elliott Kastner, the film producer, and that was a month or six weeks before my play *The Beard* opened in London, so that must have been late in '68. And I flew over to London, Jim met me at the airport, and we proceeded to do some heavy drinking.

Before we went to see Kastner, Jim and I had several days together which we spent talking about English poets and going to places like the site of William Blake's home. And in the process of talking about *The Beard*, this production of *The Beard* would have starred Jim, we decided that there was no way in 1968 that *The Beard* could be done on film without censoring it, or without radically altering the play for the film media so it could be shown.

And we decided against talking to Kastner about *The Beard*. In the meantime, Jim had read my new manuscript, my novel *The Adept*. Jim loved *The Beard* and wanted to play Billy the Kid in *The Beard*, which I thought would be beautiful. But when he read *The Adept* he said "Let's do this instead." I said, "Now that's an idea."

So before we went to see Kastner, Jim said, "Let me pitch Elliott. Let's just change projects." We arrived there, Jim with a beard and both of us with hair down to the middle of our back and pretty hung over, and god knows what Kastner thought although he was a pretty hip guy. I don't think he was exactly astonished.

So Kastner said, "What about *The Beard*?" Jim said "We've changed our mind, we want to do a new project based on Michael's novel *The Adept*." Then Jim told the story of the novel with a vivid sense of drama, great detail and full recall of what happens in it. That's complex since the novel is basically about sensory experience and it's a mystical novel…an adventure novel about an anarchist, visionary idealist coke dealer who is an outlaw motorcycle rider. Sort of a sociopathic anarchist, artist, idealist, dope dealer, back in the days in the sixties when those were real people. The characters in it are based on people I knew. People who believed in drugs, sold only certain drugs which they believed were consciousness heightening and liberating. People who were making fortunes and using their money to do things like produce plays of mine.

Michael McClure's
THE BEARD
OPENS SOON

NEWSWEEK—"A brilliant little monster of a play."

WOMEN'S WEAR DAILY—"…brutal, funny…the poetry of today…"

CUE MAGAZINE—"The author has fashioned a boisterous, very funny and novel evening."

TICKETS ON SALE AT
MUTUAL TICKET AGENCIES AND

WARNER PLAYHOUSE
755 N. La Cienega Blvd.
659-0333

PERFORMANCES: Sun., Tues., Wed., Thurs., 8:30 PM. Fri. and Sat., 8:00 PM and 10:30 PM. TWO SPECIAL NEW YEAR'S EVE PERFORMANCES. 8:00 PM and 10:30 PM.

Anyway Jim pitched the entire novel to Kastner and Kastner was interested...

Certainly Jim's intellectual abilities were stunning. I was pleased to be working with him and at that point I was just beginning to know Jim and Pam. It was a demonstration of Jim's power to recall the novel in its totality, and explain the novel to Kastner, and change it into a film as he told it, and to make it more visual for Kastner. I was impressed.

Finally Kastner passed on it. Said, "No." We were still intent on doing the novel as a film, and we were determined that we would write the script and Jim would star in it. In the meantime Jim had made contact with a man named Bill Belasco who wanted to produce it. So we talked with Bill, and we were pretty convinced that Bill could handle it. At that point Jim and I made arrangements to start writing a film script together.

I got a room at the motel across the street from The Doors' office, the Alta Cienega, where Jim always stayed. Jim was living off and on with Pam up in the glen. As much as Jim and Pam could live together they were living together, which left me in charge of the fort down at the Alta Cienega. Belasco rented an office for us on the top floor of the Scam Building. Where is it, 9000 Sunset Strip? That big glass-fronted building right in the middle of the Strip. We were on the eleventh or twelfth story, in a corner office with a couple of rooms.

Jim and I made a deal with ourselves, no drinking during the day. No drinking before work, one drink at noon, and no drinking till six o'clock, which was critical for both of us. We came in with copies of my novel and we got there by ten o'clock every morning. And Jim was never late.

He was there every morning. I was there every morning. When we first began Jim, because he'd been at UCLA film school, said, "We're going to have to do a treatment before we do the script." I said, "I don't think we're going to have to, Jim." Unfortunately we should have done the treatment.

We started working directly from the novel, just adapting the book, as it was. We got a fair distance into it, and then at that point, we were not doing what we wanted to do. Jim and I had seen many things together, both in Los Angeles and in London, that we wanted to put in the script. Jim'd say, "You remember that violinist we saw in Sloane Square, man? The kid with the rag hat?" And I'd say, "Yeah." "I want him in right here, playing down below in the street while the protagonist of *The Adept* comes to the window and looks down." I'd say, "Okay man."

Then I'd remind him of something or other and say, "Let's have that." So we started adding everything that we wanted to have in the script. It became voluminous. And we were getting ideas rapidly. Jim would shoot some of the dialogue and a twist of the plot to me or we'd go back to the book. We realized that what we were doing was that we were sitting there rapping it back and forth to each other, so we hired a secretary. She came in at ten o'clock every day too, and we started dictating to her. Jim and I would do that all day for, I don't know, three or four weeks.

We worked hard on it in such a fashion that we ended up with a script that was about the size of Moby Dick. I mean it was a couple hundred pages, and more, typed up. Then we realized what we had could not be shown to Belasco as a professional script.

In the middle of the night one night Jim cut it down to a ninety page script and he missed, he missed the point. He cut it down to the right length of a script and we had it typed up and gave it to Belasco. But I didn't like what it ended up being, because what we had originally created was a redwood tree. We created a huge script, instead of following a treatment. In a fit of creativity Jim took the redwood tree and cut it down to a ninety page toothpick. What we cut it to was not worthy of what we'd done. I think we should have begun over again following Jim's initial insight. But it didn't happen.

It could have been a wonderful film with Jim in it, it would have been beautiful.

Opposite: Backstage, Chicago, 1969.

AGILE INTELLECT

I tend to work well with people who are friends, and Jim and I worked really well. I admired the retention and the sharpness and the agility of Jim's mind. And I admired his ability considering the state that we were in at that time, because we were both alcoholic. I admired the ability that he had to cleave to the subject and stick with it. His memory was absolutely acute. He could remember, in detail, the things we'd seen together. He knew the novel so well that the novel was like a mutual experience for us.

There's a lot to say for the people you work with, when you can go away admiring them. It's not that everything is perfect, but in general you'd say, "This is a good person. This person's got a clear mind, this person's got an agile intellect, this person had good retention, this is a reasonable person, this is a strong person."

Recording his poetry, December 1970.

OH, YEAH?

When I asked Michael if he had ever seen violence in Jim, he thought for just a moment.

Oh, well. I saw him break a bottle over Babe's head. This was at that poetry conference in San Diego. Creeley was there, Dorn was there.

> **Insane weekend at college**
>   **by the sea.**
> **Sparks of car hit railing**
> **one-eyed poet by palm tree.**
> **He undresses**
> **Hit friend w/ bottle.**

(From an unpublished Morrison manuscript)

In the middle of the night, everybody was extremely intoxicated. We were sitting out on the greensward: Creeley had his clothes off and was rolling down the hill, drunkenly yelling that he was his body, it was wonderful. And Brautigan looking off into the darkness was brooding noble Brautiganian thoughts.

Jim, Babe, and I were sitting cross-legged under a tree. I don't remember what anybody was saying, but Jim reached over with an empty wine bottle and broke it over Babe's head. I said, "Jim, that was a really rotten thing to do," and he said, "Oh yeah?" And he picked up another bottle and he broke it over his own head.

So, I can't say I never saw Jim do a violent thing, but he did turn it back to himself, it was immediate self-retribution. It was shocking and very touching.

NIGGER

We went to a performance of *Paradise Now*, performed by the Living Theater in San Francisco, at the Civic Auditorium (*March 1969*). We walked in and they'd already started, and the actors were at that point where they'd stripped down and were almost nude. Remember Rufus, the black actor? Rufus let us in the door, and Jim took one look at Rufus and he yelled "Nigger" at the top of his lungs. I mean really yelled, "Nigger," loud, long, drawn out, with a lot of vehemence. And I thought, "This is crazy. The best thing to do now to protect Jim from this whole wild scene would be for me to yell nigger too," so I yelled, "Nigger" at Rufus, which made things OK because I knew Rufus pretty well and he knew me. Then we got into this thing, we started yelling nigger. It was an experience! There were hordes of sweating people in the San Francisco Civic Theater. While *Paradise Now* was going on, Jim would yell, "Rufus is a nigger." I yelled, "Judith Molina is a nigger." Jim yelled, "Nigger," and I yelled, "Julian Beck is a nigger." Jim went off the deep edge, so probably the best thing to do was join him since everyone in the Living Theater knew me and I'd been doing their theater games with them. In fact, Julian Beck was a hero for both Jim and I.

Well eventually they pushed us up on the stage. Jim was just yelling "Nigger, nigger, nigger," over and over, and I was yelling "So and so's a nigger," and "So and so's a nigger." We got to the point where we were doing those theater games, trust games, like where you'd stand on your heels and let yourself drop over backwards, then somebody catches you before you hit the floor. So we'd be yelling "Nigger" and fall straight backwards and somebody in the troupe would catch us. It went on for quite awhile. It was an amazing experience.

In the middle of this incredible scene going on, we were both totally smashed, totally raving drunk. Jim took off his jacket and he flung it out into the audience like he'd do at a Doors concert, only it was to people who didn't know who he was, and didn't know it was a $500 jacket or whatever it was. Some hand reached up like a shark and grabbed it and it was gone. But nobody in that audience there knew it was a rock star's jacket.

The next day I was sick and hung over and cleansed and fearful and trembling.

WHAT WAS HE REALLY LIKE

I asked Michael the question that is the core of the book: What was he really like?

Well I'll pass on that. That's the one like, you know, teenage kids will come up and ask you.

I said, "I've discovered there's a validity in the question and I like the simplicity of it because it really makes you condense everything you know about him into just a few honest words, a spontaneous haiku about the guy." But Michael never did answer the question, and maybe that was an answer too.

SINGING

I remember Jim sitting at my round wooden kitchen table with my wife and my daughter, and he'd start singing "House of the Rising Sun," or some Presley hit, just because he's a natural, wonderful singer. Or when we were in Chinatown, just walking down the street, Jim'd start singing some blues right out of nowhere, probably jogged by seeing some fruit in a fruit stand or catfish on cracked ice in shop window...

This was when Jim was wearing an old engineer's cap and had a beard and a pot belly, and he did it because he loved to sing. I'm not talking about a Doors song, nobody's gonna know this is Jim Morrison. Anybody would think, it's just some crazy-looking guy who's got a great voice. Right?

Performing at the Aquarius Theater, Los Angeles, 1969.

Shooting Star

What he wanted to do was make people uncomfortable with the status quo. And he did that. He did that so well, that people got angry at him.

Kathy Lisciandro and Cheri Siddons were, and still are, close friends. I hoped that by interviewing them together they would spark each other's memories and I would gain a more complete picture of Jim.

In the fall of 1969, Kathy took over the duties as secretary at The Doors office. The work included assisting Jim in many of his varied endeavors. She made clean typed drafts of his poems from the handwritten sheets and notebook pages he handed her. She took dictation and typed his letters and screened out the people he did not want to talk to on the phone. She was, as she describes it, "his literary poison taster"; he would give her screenplays and poems and other writings that came into the office and ask her to read them and recommend the ones worth his time.

Cheri knew Jim because her husband, Bill, was the band's manager. Jim could be at ease with Cheri; he knew that she would not fall victim to the stark raving infatuation that seemed to strike so many woman he came in contact with. She cared about him as a friend.

With Kathy and Cheri, Jim could explore women's mental and emotional points of view. He responded to their warm and ebullient natures; if they had a fault, it was that they occasionally acted the role of big sister and were quicker to advise and recommend conventional wisdom than he cared to hear.

Cheri Siddons, 1970.
Opposite: Jim's irresistible grin.

A LITTLE NORMALCY

CHERI: We had a very powerful, mutual affection and it was an unspoken kind of…a type of a love, I guess, a friendship love, an affection. We didn't hang out together, but when we were together there was a bond. Jim treated me as if I were very special to him and he was very special to me.

When I was pregnant with my first child, he was very curious, wanted to know what my body felt like, if there were any changes I'd noticed already. He seemed very interested in that whole process of having babies. And even after Allison was born he would always be asking me questions. He would follow me, sit next to me, with this little smirk on his face and this little gleam in his eye. He was very curious and very loving and very sweet and the last day I saw him, he was at my house and I had Allison in my lap and he sat on the floor with me and he said, "I wanted to be her godfather. Why didn't you pick me to be her godfather?"

We had an attraction, but it was almost like, "If I was some other kind of man I could have had this kind of life, I could have had this kind of woman and I could have had that baby and I could have had dinner here..." I really got that feeling that he would come and connect and have some family. A little family life, a little normalcy. I think I was a symbol of that for him.

THE SOUTHERN SHUFFLE

CHERI: He had a very unique way of walking, I don't think I could describe. He never hurried anywhere; it didn't matter if we were going to miss the plane, Jim was not hurrying. And he had an elasticity or something about him that he could be down on the floor and up and back again. He was like an acrobat or something. And then he had this quality I remember of like keeping his eyes sort of half opened and half closed. He didn't do it all the time, but I think that was the sexy look that he put on sometimes.

KATHY: The southern shuffle, is the walk. It was a slither. It was almost like he never lifted his heels off the ground, but he didn't scrape. It was a glide. Feline, sort of. But he was also clumsy at the same time. He was forever tripping up curbs, up steps, tripping over his own feet, I mean the things are sort of antithetical, but maybe because his eyes were half closed in a sexy way he couldn't see where he was going.

He spoke very slowly. It was a very deliberate way of talking as if he was thinking of what he was saying. Words just didn't fall out of his mouth without him thinking about what he was saying.

LITTLE BOY

CHERI: I remember looking at his profile a lot, and he reminded me of a cat, the way his nose was, and the way his forehead and his eyes. His eyes were kind of deep set and somehow the way the nose came down. I remember one day he was sitting next to me and I thought, "Oh my God he looks like my cat." And from that point on, I always thought he looked like a cat.

Even though he was gorgeous physically, you'd see him and know he hadn't bathed for a few days, hadn't shaved, his hair was matted. . . He didn't care about creature comforts.

Kathy and Jim in Seattle, 1970.

KATHY: There was a sense of vulnerability about him that made you want to mother him.

CHERI: Well, he was so open. And he wanted to be treated like everyone else.

KATHY: He didn't want to appear special, but being Jim he took it to extremes. The clothes he owned were basically the ones on his body at the time. Lots of times he didn't have transportation except his "feets," as he would say. He slept wherever he was at the end of the night; it could be the motel across the street, or the couch in the office, or the place he and Pamela were living at the time. So you did want to mother him and he would allow it to a certain extent. You could give him advice and then he'd go ahead and do whatever he wanted anyway.

CHERI: Absolutely.

KATHY: But he would never get angry at you for trying, so he was like a little kid, a lot like a little boy at times who was disobeying. I'm going to get away with this whether you like it or not.

CHERI: He had a lot of the petulant child, the impish, mischievous child in him, the prankster, sometimes. Let's push and prod and see what we can get this human being to do, and how we can get this other person to react.

KATHY: He was a clown. Yes. He liked getting away with stuff. He enjoyed himself as much as he could. I think he found himself, a lot of times, in situations that he really didn't want to be in, but there was no way out for him. So the only way he could cope was, "Well, let's see how far I can take this," and "How much can I get away with. Let's take it to the limit and see what happens from there." And when you're there, well, let's go that next step and see what happens. And he did that with everything. In all aspects of his life.

SPOON RINGS

CHERI: I remember one time we were having dinner in a restaurant and some young girls came in. They were walking by and they looked in the window and they came up and asked Jim for his autograph in the middle of the meal. And he was his polite southern gentleman person, "Where are you from, what's your name," that kind of thing. Talked to them for maybe ten minutes and they went away just ecstatically happy.

KATHY: And that sense of politeness…not even politeness, this is a real kindness. We were at lunch and a street vendor came by, a young kid, and he had a cigar box filled with spoon rings which at the time were very popular. A spoon ring is a ring that's made out of the handle end of an old spoon and it usually has a design on it. People would chop off that end and then bend it around to make a ring out of it.

So this kid came by with a cigar box filled with rings and he came to our table and asked if Jim wanted to buy one. Jim looked at me right away and said, "Take one for yourself," and I said, "Great, thanks." So I picked one out and the guy was ready to walk away, thrilled that he made this sale, but Jim called him back and said, "How much for the whole box?" The kid nearly died. Jim found some money in his pockets and handed it to him, and the kid gave him the box of rings. I still have mine.

Kathy's spoon ring.

ANTAGONISM

Cheri, as the wife of the band's manager, and Kathy, as the office secretary, each had a unique vantage point to view Jim's relationship with the other members of the band.

KATHY: It seemed to me that he was always distant with them. I never saw him be rude or nasty or yell at them. In fact I never heard Jim raise his voice, except when he was singing or on stage. He always seemed to deal with the other three in a very…he wanted to get it over with in a very businesslike way, as quickly as possible, and at a distance. That seemed to be the way he handled The Doors.

Even in social situations when, for one reason or another, we were all together at a party or a dinner or whatever, he never really seemed to socialize with them in a personal kind of way.

CHERI: As far as being on the stage, he always wanted to be introduced as The Doors, not Jim Morrison and The Doors. That seemed to be very

Cheri listens to a Doors rehearsal, 1970.

important to him. But I can see them standing here and him standing there, almost like it was an invisible line. I felt that the three of them were a unit and he wasn't part of that unit.

KATHY: I think there was always a sense of antagonism. They were never sure what Jim was going to do. Whether he was going to show up for a gig on time; and if he did show up whether he was going to be drunk. And that made them totally insecure about where their next paycheck was coming from. I think it came down a lot to business...

CHERI: Responsibility also. I mean they had a responsibility to perform and they didn't know what condition he would arrive in. He usually did arrive, but it was quite often late, at the last second. Most of us were going, "Oh, God, where is he, is he coming?" and I think sometimes they'd get on stage and they'd be angry and they'd have to get through that anger in the performance. I began to see a split as time went on.

KATHY: And over the years, because it became such a big business, their attitude about it changed. Jim always wanted it to be the small club, new material, that sense of maybe making a difference in some form or another with his words, and with a real personal relationship between the band members and him, and him and the band with the audience. As you perform in larger and larger venues you lose that sense of intimacy, not only with the audience but with your own material. Jim constantly fought that. The other three guys just went along with it because they saw more business. Money didn't matter to Jim the way it mattered to the others.

CHERI: He was an artist. And I think the angriest he ever was happened when The Doors decided to let Buick use "Light My Fire." I just remember this real unhappiness. I think if he ever was going to yell, he would have yelled that day. He didn't yell, but to me it was almost like a light switched off. That was like the last straw somehow.

I'm not so sure if he really liked Robby, Ray, and John after that. I think he could sense they had different purposes; they were more into the money and the business and would sacrifice some of the art for that. Jim was not willing to sacrifice the art for anything.

CHUBBY

He tried to give the audience what he thought they expected, and I think he gave them everything he had to give. It was almost like it was a place for him to share his deepest self. It drove people crazy, people loved it. And then I think it got to the point where he didn't know why he was doing it anymore, or what anybody really wanted of him.

I remember one time—it was before the Long Beach concert and we were sitting backstage, and in those days the backstage wasn't the massive scene of people that it is now. Jim and I were sitting there and you could hear the crowd screaming, "Jim, Jim, Jim!" and he just looked over at me and said, "What do they want from me? I don't know what they want from me."

I think he just wanted to be accepted for the human being that he was, and he knew that masses of people couldn't accept him as a one-on-one human being. They couldn't separate the performance from the human that was giving the performance. That eventually caused him to grow a beard, get chubby and say, "See if they accept me like this!"

UNCOMFORTABLE WITH THE STATUS QUO

KATHY: There was a real dichotomy in his personality, his stage personality and "himself," who he really was as a person. The press only saw the stage personality, because that's all he'd let them see. And then as his fame grew, as his more outrageous antics on stage and off were reported in the press, the momentum was so great that it overwhelmed the personal side of his personality. There was no way that Jim could redeem himself anymore.

What he wanted to do was make people uncomfortable with the status quo. And he did that. He did that so well, that people got angry at him, and did not want to hear what he had to say.

CHERI: But what the fans loved about him was that he was moving and shaking, he was making changes.

KATHY: The fans were young kids, teenagers, who listened to what he was saying. Who didn't mind having the status quo shaken up, who wanted to hear something different and new. They were totally unsatisfied with the world, with what was going on at the time.

AMSTERDAM '68

CHERI: I never thought of Jim as a drug addict; I always thought he was an alcoholic. Maybe I wouldn't have labeled him "an alcoholic," but I knew that he drank far too much and I knew that drinking was his problem.

We were in Amsterdam, sitting in the audience watching the Jefferson Airplane and all of a sudden Jim came out and did his little snake dance. Everybody loved it and the audience thought it was wonderful but you could tell that he wasn't quite in control. I went backstage when the Airplane went off and Jim started getting really sick.

Everybody else was standing there going, "Oh, God, he's sick," and sort of wanting to be away from him. Billy was trying to decide what to do. He thought that if he got Jim some oxygen that Jim could still go on. I knew that Jim wasn't going on, but Billy always thought ...I don't know...So the ambulance came and they weren't about to just give him oxygen, they took him to the hospital.

The next day the rest of The Doors went on to the next venue and Billy and I stayed on and we went to the hospital and we saw Jim and we talked to the doctor and the doctor said, "This guy's liver is really not good. If he doesn't stop the drinking, he's not going to live."

That was September 1968.

Opposite: Jim sings "Wishful, Sinful," New York City, May 1969.

SHE BRINGS THE SUN
So I asked them, "What was he really like?"

KATHY: I don't think you ever really know what someone else is *really* like, no matter how long or how well you know someone. From what I knew and felt Jim was a real friend; he was kind, he was gentle, he was extraordinarily generous, he was willing to give you anything that you wanted or anything that you asked for, and he liked it better when he could offer.

Times when he knew that I was alone in town for a while by myself, he would say, if you ever need anything, give me a call. Or if you have to do this, let me know. He made it known that he was there for me if I needed him.

He was probably one of the most intelligent people I've ever met. Extraordinarily well read. But there was a sense of intelligence about him that went beyond the academic. There was that sense of philosophical curiosity that had nothing to do with book learning. There was a sense of wiseness and maturity that he had about him that goes beyond a university degree.

CHERI: A knowingness, I think.

KATHY: And a sense of curiosity about the world that surpassed anyone else that I knew at the time. It wasn't just the degree from UCLA and what he learned out of books or the titles in his library, which were extensive, but that sense of self-knowledge that went beyond what most people at that age, at that time, would even begin to think about.

Sometimes when I was typing up his poems, I'd come across a word and I didn't know what it meant, and I'd say what does this mean? And he would give me the history of the word. If that word was specific to something, he would give me some of the history that was going on around the time, so I would have an idea really what that word meant in time and space. That kind of knowledge, that kind of book learning.

CHERI: I agree, he was extremely intelligent. He was also soft, and he was funny. I felt protected when he was around, I don't know what that means, but I somehow felt protected.

I remember walking into the office one day, I opened the door and went walking in and there were people sitting on the couch and Jim was there and he said, "Look at her, she brings the sun into the room." He used to say wonderful things.

He was the most powerfully charismatic human being I've ever met and probably ever will meet. Somewhere I heard the line, "shooting star," you know, people who come here for a short time and they do their work and they leave, and as soon as I heard that I understood exactly that it applied to Jim.

THIRTY

How do they explain Jim's attraction to ledges and edges?

KATHY: I think he was a thrill-seeker,…but with a purpose. I think he was a thrill-seeker because he wanted to experience as much as he possibly could. His seekings had more of a sense of purpose to them than wanton acts of self-destruction. I never felt that…I don't think he was self-destructive in that sense. So that when he did put himself in danger, I think he really had a purpose. What that purpose was, I don't know.

CHERI: On his twenty-fifth birthday we were walking down the stairs of The Doors office and he said to me, "Well, I made it to 25, do you think I'll make it to 30?" And we both knew he wouldn't make it to 30.

Surrounded by fans after a concert in Los Angeles, 1967.

A Cosmic Spanking

...he gave her something that she'll remember forever, he gave her what she was asking about, he gave her a little cosmic spanking.

A *photographer, painter, and writer, Leon Barnard still lives the same kind of outdoor existence he had before he met up with Jim Morrison and tried on, for awhile, the role of publicist for a rock 'n' roll band. Nothing much has changed, he says; he leads a very simple life.*

I had a studio down in Long Beach, California and a friend of mine, Charlie Hawkins, showed up one night with a friend of his, Bill Siddons, on their motorcycles. I had been evicted from my studio and had to leave, so I had tickets to go to Europe the following day, April 1, 1968.

Charlie and Bill and I drank some beer and smoked some dope together and sat around and giggled for a couple of hours and then when they were leaving, Bill said that maybe the next time he saw me would be in Denmark because he was coming over in September. So I gave him my phone number and said give me a call when you get there and he gave me his business card which said "The Doors, Management." I was shocked, blown away by it so I said, "You manage The Doors?" They had just hired him two weeks before. He said, "The group's going to do their first European tour in September." So jokingly I said, "Well, I'll promote you," meaning I'll go around and tell all my friends about it.

I called him the next day and I said I really would like to promote the band, figuring, well, maybe if I did a good job they'd let me come backstage or give me free tickets or ride around in a limousine or something.

Leon at his desk in The Doors office, 1969.
Opposite: Jim at the Hollywood Bowl, July 1968.

Bill told Leon to go for it and gave him a handful of press materials.

I went around Copenhagen for the next three months barefoot, wearing cutoffs and a T-shirt and introducing myself as the European representative for The Doors. And when I said it I believed it, I pictured it, and I became it.

Leon achieved results and he sent long letters back to The Doors' office in West Hollywood humorously detailing his adventures and accomplishments.

Anyway, I went on to Sweden and then to Germany and then ended up in England and hitchhiked to the Roundhouse Chalk Farm (*a large indoor arena*). And when I walked into the Roundhouse, Bill turned and saw me, opened up his arms, came, embraced me, put his

Asbury Park, 1968.

hands on my shoulders, and said, "The guys really like you, here's some money, their limousine's out in front, we're staying at the Royal Lancaster Hotel. You're doing our European tour." The Doors were on stage rehearsing. That was my first glimpse of the band and the first time I ever saw Jim Morrison.

The next morning we were outside the lobby on the street with limousines waiting to take us to rehearsal. And I was reading *Melody Maker* when I saw the cowboy boots, and then the leather pants, and then the white lacy shirt and then looked up and saw the angelic face of Jim Morrison. I made eye contact with him, and he reached out and said, "Hi, I'm Jim," and I said, "My name's Leon." And he said, "Oh, you're the guy in Copenhagen. Get in, I want to hear about the Danish people."

So I rode with him and Pam and he interviewed me during the twenty minute ride to find out what the Danish people were like. He asked me if I ever wore shoes because I was barefoot. And he wanted to know if my feet got cold or if I ever cut them by stepping on things. He was genuinely interested in what I was all about and at that point a kind of a friendship took place. There was a sincerity about him, a truthfulness.

THE WALK & THE TALK

Jim lived in his cowboy boots; he sometimes slept in them. And he wore tight leather pants so they restricted his movement, and then, of course, when you wear cowboy boots it causes you to saunter rather than to take strides. I described it as almost like a geisha girl taking small steps in a tight skirt. So he sauntered with small steps and whereas other people walk, Jim Morrison just kind of glided along not lifting his feet

Jim often stood close to Ray or Robby, watching their fingers produce the music. It was as if he could see the notes.

very high off the ground. And Jim didn't run to catch airplanes—he was never in a hurry— and he never sensed that there was any state of emergency.

If I speak at 55 miles an hour, Jim probably spoke at 25 or 30. He spoke slowly. His movements were systematic and deliberate, calculated in a sense. He was very aware of words and the impact that they would have and he selected them carefully, thoughtfully, and then reported them slowly in a dreamy kind of way.

INTERVIEWS

Leon arranged press interviews and he stood by while they were being conducted, in case of trouble.

I would say one of the best ones, I believe, was with Tony Thomas from Canadian Broadcasting. He approached the interview in a professional manner; he was dressed in a business suit and he gave directions for Jim and me where to sit and how to sit, and to pull the chair forward.

Tony opened the interview with, "…your new book of poems…" and as soon as he said that Jim's ears perked up and you could feel the purr, this man wants to talk about my poetry and not necessarily about record albums or concerts or jail sentences. And there was a rapport that was developed. Mutual respect right away.

Tony Thomas: Jim, in the very first line of your new book of poems, it reads "Look where we worship." What do young people worship today? What do they believe? What do they hang onto, what do they hope for?

Jim: Well, I can't speak for young people but probably a guess would be the same things they've always celebrated, just kind of a joy of existence, self discovery, freedom, that kind of thing.

COSMIC ORGASM
Not all interviews went so smoothly.

Lita Elisque came out from New York to do an interview with him. We went to the Garden District to do the interview and she began to ask him the usual questions. And then she asked him a question about the leather pants and his persona, and did that carry into his bedroom activity. So Jim said, "Well, yeah. I like to use a hairbrush every now and then." Well, her eyes lit up because she's doing something for *Look Magazine*, but she could see it being divided and some of it going to *The Village Voice*, too.

And she began asking him all the provocative questions about his sex life. So Jim started telling her, making up stories, I mean he was telling her things that I hadn't imagined yet. And he went on for about fifteen minutes. She asked him how many girls he'd ever slept with. And he said he thought about 1,000. And then she asked him out of 1,000 how many cosmic orgasms do you think? And he said well probably about one out of 1,000 girls.

He gave her all this juicy information and then when it had reached its conclusion, he reached over and grabbed the tape recorder. While she's protesting, he pulled the tape out and he gave it to me. She's going, "You motherfucker, I'm going to sue you, I have a copyright to that." And he said, "Leon, can you guarantee me that you'll erase this tape and give it back to her?" And I said, "It's done." She's screaming, "Motherfucker!" I went back to the office, erased the tape, took it to the Beverly Hills Hotel, gave her the blank tape. She had nothing to write except what was left in her memory. I felt that he gave her something that she'll remember forever, he gave her what she was asking about, he gave her a little cosmic spanking.

Opposite: Waiting to go through customs in Canada.

THE DESK AND THE BAND

Jim was one of the great publicists, one of the great press agents of the world. I mean, I usually tell people that he was his own press agent. He's the one that came up with the ideas, and I was more or less the messenger or the delivery boy for those ideas.

I loved it when Jim used to say, "Oh, oh, I'm getting a cerebral erection." And then he'd hold his hands to his head because he had a new idea for a poem or song and then laugh about it. It was the laughter that followed that was wonderful.

He had requested a desk and we actually postponed getting it for a while. We took our time in getting it because we didn't realize how important it was to him. And then Bill and Kathy went out and found him a desk. My desk was a big desk although it was used and funky, and Bill's was a sizable desk and Kathy had a nice-sized desk. All we were able to find Jim was a small student desk.

We put his own telephone line in for him and his pen and pencil and everything so he could have a little focus where he could sit and write his notes and make his telephone calls, and he seemed to take it very personally. It seemed to be his piece of real estate even though he didn't own a car at the time and he didn't own a house and the only belongings that he had were the things that he wore on his body at the moment. The desk was definitely his own, and on occasions, when he slept in the office…We had a real comfortable sofa and the first one that got to the office got the sofa, so if I was in first, I got the sofa and then he would curl up on the floor underneath his own little desk.

And if other people came to sit at his desk he had a sense of being guarded about it, an initial sense of being guarded about it but eventually he would acquiesce as a special favor to a friend. And it's almost as though he laid claim to that little piece of property.

He'd spend time at the desk when he was in town. He doodled and he telephoned, he read his fan mail and he wrote notes and then oftentimes, too, his desk was right across from Kathy so there was a direct line of communication as far as talking with her about how he wanted to transcribe his poetry. It offered him a little sense of family and camaraderie to be a part of the office.

The downstairs part of the building was of course their, the band's, workshop, and you know I'm almost sure that Jim Morrison functioned for the couple of years that I was around him (*from September 1968 to June 1970*) almost out of a sense of adversity towards the other group members.

I think there was tension between the three group members and Jim because of his bad-boy image or his antics. There wasn't a lot of love focused among them like there might have been in the beginning days. There was something about them that he resented. They came together and made music for a few hours but it wasn't a place that any of them were fond of being after it was over. It's let's do it together and then I'm

Opposite: Jim at an anti-war demonstration in Venice, California, 1969.

going to go over here with my buddies and you're going to go over to where you're going.

And sometimes on stage you could see that kind of adversity taking place, a kind of anger that developed that. . . that Jim provoked from time to time. He liked teasing them.

On tour with The Doors. Left to right: Tony Funches, Jim, Leon and Kathy.

WALK AWAY

Although Jim was interested in the details of other people's lives, he rarely revealed his own background. Sometimes it was difficult to get him to talk about yesterday, but he would share his thoughts of the future.

The time that he and Kathy and I had lunch together at the Garden District, the last time that I saw him, he began talking about changing his identity and the fact that he was maturing at the age of twenty-seven and that he viewed things differently. I got the feeling that he was closer to being Jim Morrison as a mature adult, that he was unhappy with performing for "bubble-gummers" (those were his words). There was a little bit of pain; he felt that he was not fully appreciated as an intellectual, or as a poet. He said that the longevity of a rock 'n' roll group was five years and that they had reached that peak. That's why later I felt that he was contemplating a disappearance because you can go for five years and then, after that, you become just another one of the general public.

And he said that Pamela was the one who had gotten under his skin, that she was his cosmic mate. He considered her to be his cosmic counterpart. He felt that he couldn't live without her, that she was the one that he always returned to and she was the complement to his existence, that he was considering going to Paris and writing screenplays and giving up the whole superstar persona thing, that it had now reached its conclusion. That was an existential move to be able to turn away, to walk away from it.

Chris Boyle had seen The Doors in Tulsa as a high school senior and had written a piece about them for his school paper. When he came to California, he continued to pursue his interests in music and journalism. He called Leon at The Doors' office on a daily basis with suggestions and offers of help. Eventually he got himself hired.

Chris: The first time I met Jim was on October 8, 1967 at the Tulsa Civic Center Auditorium at their concert, which was one week after their national appearance on *The Ed Sullivan Show.* I was back stage and Jim turned to me as he walked into the dressing room alone and said, "We'd like to be alone now." So I closed the door and left, realizing he was the only one in there and that he had said we. Now that I think about it, he was right. There were "we's" contained in the singular body of Jim Morrison. He wasn't the only person or spirit inside his body. He was a writer, reader, poet, songwriter, singer, entertainer, rock star, legend, shaman...

BUCK OWENS

An intelligent and curious young man, Chris observed Jim Morrison with special interest during the times they were in the office together.

Jim was a sponge. He soaked up everything—books, words, songs, information, life, death, sex, drugs, alcohol. He soaked it all up and retained it for his own creative powers.

Jim had just returned from New York. He had brought back a small cardboard box full of records he had collected. Kathy, Leon, Bill, and I were in the office working on this day and Jim asked me to pick out an album and put on some music. Not wanting to disappoint him and also wanting to see if I could blow his mind, I looked for something real weird and corny. I saw this album called *No Ambulance Tonight Niggers.* I wasn't sure. When I saw *Buck Owens and the Buckaroos Live in London* I thought, that's it. I put it on the turntable.

"Turn it up," Jim said. I did and he yelled, "Louder, Chris." Bill Siddons was the first one to get annoyed. "Are you guys makin' enough noise out there?" he yelled from the inner sanctum of his office, adding, "You know, there are some people in this office who are trying to work."

Then he slammed his door. Jim laughed and I snickered a little, but Kathy and Leon looked upset. All of a sudden Bill rushed out of the office saying he was going to lunch. Leon said he couldn't hear anything and he was leaving. He and Kathy went to lunch. That left Jim and I and Buck. "Turn it up, Chris," Jim said.

I kept going back into Bill's office to the refrigerator and bringing out the beers, and we kept playing the record louder and louder, and Jim and I were singing all the words until we had it memorized.

The best part was on the last song where Buck slows it down, gospel style and talks about how his grandmother was dyin' and asked him to play this song. It's a real sobbin' tear jerkin' intro and song. Jim and I had our arms over each other's shoulders as we talked and sang along with Buck. It was amazing how fast Jim memorized every line.

GET UP AND DO SOMETHING

> There are no longer "dancers," the possessed.
> The cleavage of men into actor and spectators
> is the central fact of our time. We are obsessed
> with heroes who live for us and whom we punish.
> If all the radios and televisions were deprived
> of their sources of power, all books and paintings
> burned tomorrow, all shows and cinemas closed,
> all the arts of vicarious existence . . .
>
> We are content with the 'given' in sensation's
> quest. We have been metamorphosed from a mad
> body dancing on hillsides, to a pair of eyes
> staring in the dark.

(from *The Lords*)

When Jim was in Tulsa and I saw him perform, he said, "Hey you out there," and he was pointing to the guy in the fourth row, and he started laughing this really evil laugh, and he says, "You out there, you are alone and want to dance and nobody can help you," and he just laughed.

Now, lookin' back, I realize that he wasn't just pointing at that one guy, he was speaking basically to a whole generation of people. The fact that people would just sit and watch and simply be entertained, and they would consider that living. And it satisfied them. He saw that as kind of a sick thing. And to him…he was a person who preached and acted totally the opposite. He wanted…he was a mad body dancing on a hillsides, he wasn't a pair of eyes staring in the dark. His message was get up and do something.

Opposite: During his performances in 1967, like this one in Tulsa, Oklahoma, Jim was animated from the first note to the last chord.

This Affair of Ours

...they would rush up to the stage and he would lash out with his microphone, like an animal tamer, just scream at them, "Shut up! Sit down!"

*A*t some point during their stay in the City of Angels, just about everyone in this story, including Jim, lived in the hills spreading out and up from Laurel Canyon Boulevard. Driving through the canyon on my way to talk to Eva, I noticed someone had scrawled graffiti on the house in which Jim and Pam lived, the one behind the country store that he sings about in "Love Street." The house is being repaired or remodeled and its ribs show through in some places; in white fourteen inch-high letters the grafittist has painted, MR. MOJO RISIN'.

In her native Hungary, Eva went to law school. She came to live in the United States in 1967 as the new bride of the documentary filmmaker Frank Gardonyi, who had fled Hungary during the 1956 uprising. Like the rest of us, Jim was smitten by Eva's Central European earthiness and beauty. He felt at ease wiiith this educated and widely traveled woman who saw him as another admirer and a friend.

Eva learned to read English with comic books and pornographic novels, and her command of idiomatic English, even in the sixties when she was first speaking the language, has always been impressive. I cannot reproduce the sensual husky timbre of her voice nor her captivating Hungarian accent, but I can reproduce her exact words and sentences. Written English might suffer, but this is meant to be conversation, and Eva has a wonderfully fresh way of expressing herself. I asked her to tell me about the first time she met Jim.

Eva, 1970

I recall that I found him very shy and very self-editing. It was strange because before I met him I heard the stories about him and

I was ready to meet this incredibly out-of-control, crazed man. When I met him I was surprised how quiet, how observant he was. He's just looking every place, checked and double checked everything what was going on.

Because Americans are usually outgoing and although he had a tremendous presence, in his demeanor he was very, very shy and spoke very little and always sort of sat aside. I heard that he would do all sorts of outrageous things and I was always looking for when he's going to piss on the floor or something which never happened. In fact, there were times when you guys would come over to our house, and all three of you were obviously a little loaded, but never ever did anything out of line, which I just couldn't even understand.

TWO SUITCASES

I don't know if you ever knew about that…us living together? Nobody really knew he was there. When Frank left…(*Eva's husband, Frank, packed up and left for Mexico one day, and it was the end of their relationship. A few weeks before Pam had gone off to Europe, leaving Jim alone in LA.*)…the same night Jimmy moved in and lived there with me for about a month and a half, two months.

So Frank left at five in the afternoon, at eleven o'clock somebody's knocking on the door, and I opened the door and there's Jimmy and he's got two suitcases. The taxi's pulling away. It was quite funny…with suitcases 'cause he never travelled with anything, as you know.

And the way he conducted himself at that point, it must have taken him a lot of drinking, or I don't know what it was, but where to get the nerve that he would do it. And as soon as I opened the door he put his feet in there like he wasn't sure that I'm gonna let him in, and he kept like pushing me back toward the room saying I love you, I love you, and he didn't stop doing that until he got me into bed.

I mean it was like he left the suitcases somewhere in the living room and ended up in my bedroom, but it was very bold.

And I never assumed that he had any interest because he was always like such a gentleman. Never any indication of him being interested in that way.

I was surprised, I was flattered, and I was stoned. I don't know, all these together and, yeah, it surprised me that he took the opportunity and he had the guts since his suitcases were with him.

He said for a long time before he had a crush on me, which I didn't know but…

Well, I was flirtatious. I flirted with just about everybody, yeah.

Jimmy was a wonderful person to be with because he was giving. He was giving of his time, of his attention. He would focus and listen to you and have a conversation, not like surface conversations.

He enjoyed playing house. Yeah, he enjoyed that. He just so many times said it's so nice to have like dinner and be home and just lock the door and he liked that.

Our lifestyle was somehow not to get together with people. When we had a little time together we wouldn't just party it up because he was working on the damn record. So all his afternoons were spent in the recording studios and then he would be back. It would be sometimes quite late and we would stay up to four, five in the morning, let the sun come up.

ETHICAL

He was feeling extremely anxious about this affair of ours because he liked Frank. He felt very bad even though Frank already made the decision and moved out. And that's why, that was the reason that he wanted to keep it sort of quiet because he felt guilty about it in a funny way. See he was so ethical. You know how ethical he was. He did this outrageousness and everything but still that wasn't done in his book and he was doing it and it didn't make him extremely proud.

At the same time he had this outrageous nature, too, and it can go together very easily because that has nothing to do with your ethical being. It is something of a personality trait.

STOP EVERYTHING

Occasionally he would stop everything he was doing and pull out a notebook and start writing in it, and it would be poetry. He was very much aware of himself being a poet and apparently a good poet, you know, so he found it very important whenever he had the urge to take the time.

In fact, he spent a lot of his time writing, and it was understood then that he's writing poetry. He read me a couple of his poems but in general he wouldn't tell me about all the poetry he was writing. Ours was a different relationship.

He went to sleep very badly because he drank and then he became insomniac, you know, afraid he couldn't sleep. While he was in this insomniac state was he writing.

We took a very interesting acid trip together but he wrote profusely all night long. But often, very often, there were these moments where he would find something either that I said or what just happened, and then he would have to write something about it.

He wasn't as much sharing about the poems as his music. When he came back from whatever he was doing every night that's the first thing was that he put on his records. He liked to listen to his records, and he listened to them with this major interest, and he sang with his records. He loved to sing to his music. I always found it very amusing how fresh it always was to him.

And he was singing the stuff that he was recording at that time, too, the "LA Woman" record, and asking me about them and everything, but majorly just being satisfied more or less with, you know, the music.

I didn't go to the recording sessions. I didn't like those things. Besides which we kind of kept us a secret. It was very sexy that way. We went to movie theaters sometimes and took drives.

BITCHING & MOANING

When coming home from recording and everything he would be full of momentary complaints and bitching and excitement or whatever. He would bring it all home and share it…yeah.

And about these other three musicians I never heard anything but complaining from him. He was frustrated with members of his group. He was bitching and moaning about them a lot and hardly can wait when he's gonna be on his own. That's all, well, but of course it was tainted with some major arguments and everything…in recording studios for eight, ten, twelve hours so, that's what I would hear about.

You know, well by that time he wasn't on good terms with any of them and he was deeply disappointed with all of them.

Opposite: Listening to Ray's solo at the Hollywood Bowl, July 5, 1968. Following: The Doors, joined by Jerry Scheff on bass and Marc Benno on rhythm guitar during a recording session for LA Woman.

SINGING IN THE MIRROR

The way he looked at himself in a mirror I think he was very pleased with his own appearance. I think he could look really lovingly in the mirror and look at himself. I mean there was no problem. I think he wasn't a vain person, he wasn't into looking pretty at that point of his life.

And all these teenage girls idolizing him, this sex image in the magazines, I mean he was always like pushing it aside. No...that was just ridiculous for him as far as I could see. If he had any images of himself as such he did not discuss it, most certainly. But he was very gracious when we met up with fans. We went a couple of times to movies or something and then when we would come out fans would run up to him and ask him for interviews and just like, "Jim, Jim!" and he was always taking out a little time to be nice and, you know, did a little PR job. And that was amazing, too, because he did have the patience for that and liked it.

And in fact I think at that point he missed...because his star was falling at that point he felt...he was grateful for recognition.

PAMELA

Sometimes when she was angry, I guess, she'd curse him but never, ever thought of him as a bad poet. Oh, she thought of him as a wonderful poet.

She was quick, Pamela, and she was...she had a clarity of a child with very good intuitions, and an innocence that Jimmy loved in her a great deal. That childish innocence. She was easy to burst into laughter and look at life in that love child, you know, that sweet child manner.

Jimmy said, "She was a child when we met and I always feel responsible for her because she sort of never grew up." He felt that he would have to take care of her the rest of his life because they started together. She was there when he had to just do it out of nothing and from no-

where and she believed in him and he appreciated that. I know that they had been starving together and that was a very important thing. Not when he had money or not when he had fame but prior to that. They'd known each other and supported each other and you know he was certainly having responsibilities with her.

And he forgave her a lot of things. And even though she was at times impossible to be with, he would say, "She's a sweet child." Somehow he just needed to take care of her. Actually it was quite touching. She was one of the few people he trusted enough to bare himself.

She always gave him quite a lot of attention and admiration, and he also showed a great deal of kindness and loving behavior toward her. And they argued, you know, they both had their grievances, like "you done that to me and for that I done that to you."

Somehow they always seemed to have gravitated back to each other after every little escapade, you know.

Pamela Courson and Jim in 1968. The photos on these pages are from Pam's own photo album.

HOUR OF THE WOLF

Directly after the concert in Miami Jim flew to Jamaica for a planned vacation that was supposed to include Pam, but they argued before Jim left Los Angeles and she refused to go with him. On the island, Jim stayed in a big house all alone. Save for the black Jamaicans who were there to look after his welfare, he was completely isolated. Afterwards, in a long poem entitled "Jamaica," he described a vacation that became a nightmare.

> The hour of the wolf
> has now ended. Cocks
> crow. The world is built
> up again, struggling in
> darkness.
>
> The child gives in to night-
> Mare, while the grown
> Man fears his fear.
>
> I must leave this island,
> Struggling to be born
> from blackness.

(from "Jamaica" as published in Wilderness)

One day he was telling us how frightened he was in Jamaica and Pamela sat up sort of indignant saying how come I've never known about these things before and he just smiled you know and he said, "Well I don't talk about everything all the time."

He told us they took him down there, down to apparently a palazzo, a mansion, and there were like black servants and everything and he said that he was very much afraid of these black people at that point because they looked so foreign and alien to him and everything. And apparently the rest of the group got into other households. They just left him alone. And then this guy, this butler or whatever he was, this black guy, pulled out a bunch of dope and he offered to roll him a joint. Jim said it was like a cigar and he started smoking it a little bit and he didn't like smoking, or didn't smoke that much or whatever, but it affected him in the weirdest way 'cause he started like hallucinating that people are going to kill him and this guy's after him and everything.

He said it was almost like visions. You know when you have a bad trip you know you just see negative and scary in everything. And since the circumstances were such that he found himself alone in this huge mansion with a couple of rasta guys hanging around, he just didn't know how to read it and he felt that it was somewhat of a conspiracy or something.

And he would call Robbie and, I don't know, John, to come and like fetch him and those guys didn't want anything to do with him. They were pissed off, they were mad from what happened in Miami and everything and so they really isolated him. He said he had the worst time on that island. Riddled with like fear and disappointment and loneliness and everything. . .

That was a very fearful experience for him and it got in touch with his relationship with blacks because he said he didn't trust them. He didn't understand them. He said, "I was like a white boy not knowing my place in this thing."

MAGICIAN

I heard this incredible bad reputation sort of foreshadowed and then nothing of the sort came out. Only when I'd see his strength was when he was on stage.

My impression of Jim on stage was absolute amazement because, as I told you, I had met this very shy and timid and always smiling Jimmy with no visible strength whatsoever. And then I saw him on stage performing "Light My Fire," and all these numbers of his and his command of his audience was startling. I remember him commanding these, how many thousands and thousands of people, they would rush up to the stage and then he would lash out with his microphone and like an animal tamer, you know, just scream at them, "Shut up! Sit down!" and everybody, like puppies, would march back to their chairs. I'd never seen a single man handle people like that at that magnitude, you know. He was like a black magician, I was almost frightened of him, his strength.

DON'T KILL ME

People say he was self-destructive and talk about all he might have been, but he loved living and he had great plans for living. Furthermore, when I drove recklessly he would hang onto the car saying, "Oh, don't kill me, you know I love living."

No Future & No Past

I just think he was trapped somewhere in a persona he didn't envision for himself and there he was.

*O*f all the people who knew Jim and spent time with him during the last years of his life, no one was closer to him than Babe Hill. With mischievous eyes, a full curly beard, sunbleached hair worn to his shoulders, and sturdy build, Babe was usually mistaken for an outlaw biker. Definitely someone you would not want to mess with.

Babe worked on both of Jim's films, Feast of Friends *and* HWY *and he delighted Jim with a carefree manner, quick verbal wit and keen intelligence. By 1969, the team of Morrison and Hill was well established and they were constant companions.*

What was Babe doing before he joined up with Jim?

I was in Virginia working on a survey ship, I was a hydrographic surveyor. I just came out of a very straight line existence. The Viet Nam war and all of that stuff was going way over my head, stuff I was seeing on TV. I was still a young kid, even though I was married and had a kid. I was just interested in doing my work, going to the bar, and playing pool.

I broke up with my old lady, I dropped out and I hooked up with Paul (*Paul Ferrara was then working for The Doors as their still photographer*), an old high school and junior high buddy. We ran into each other and he said, "I'm just moving up here in the mountains, if you want, come up and stay with me." That was January 1968.

And at that time there were people living on the streets and they had causes and ideas. It was all kind of new to me, and I was getting off behind it. I had just recently dropped out and I was still trying to tune in, turn on.

One of the main things I was interested in was LSD, not as a trip but as a serious psychological tool. I had been out of touch for a long

Above: Babe Hill, 1970.
Opposite: Jim fishes off the coast of the Bahamas, 1970.

time, and in the meanwhile Jim and everyone else at UCLA had been doing acid for a couple of years.

There was an aura of hopefulness in the air, the Viet Nam war aside. There was an expectation of change brewing, definitely, and revolution, but a gentle, hopeful revolution about humanitarian things, issues. Not worldwide political issues.

ROWDY

By the middle of July 1968 when I started working on Feast of Friends *(the film) Jim had established a kind of drinking and partying relationship with Babe, who he could trust to stay with him until the end of the evening and sometimes straight through to the dawn.*

Jim and I were so different. Our backgrounds were so different. Being rowdy to me was going to a beer bar and playing pool and getting into fights. Jim could come along and watch that stuff but he couldn't really join in with it.

When we'd go to San Francisco and hang out with Michael (*Michael McClure*) and go to his plays and things like that, we'd just get loud and joyous and happy and cheering and all that kind of stuff in the theater. Jim didn't hold back when he wanted to. He could be that way: loud and happy.

He had a good sense of humor, he had a great sense of humor. He loved to laugh, he laughed all the time. I remember if something humorous would happen around the office, he'd get a big guffaw out of it. I would say that he definitely had an exuberant personality. He was not morose.

THE BLUE LADY

In all the years I knew him, Jim only owned one car, a Ford Shelby GT-500, an American muscle car of awesome power. Babe, showing his romantic and poetic nature, named her the Blue Lady after a character in Jim's "Hitchhiker" scenario. Too often after a night of heavy drinking Jim would slip behind the wheel and scare his passengers to prayers.

Well, I remember one night in the Blue Lady, we went racing down some street. He just took off and the street ended, it dead ended. Jim was drunk and we had Violet, one of our cocaine queens, with us. I was just holding on to her, man. I said, "Here we go, we're going to die."

And he hit the brakes and we went over the curb and we went up on the lawn and we dead ended against a tree. It just so happened we were right in the back of the Beverly Hills Police Dept.

It didn't wreck the car but it more or less wiped out the undercarriage pretty well. We hit the curb straight on. It wasn't a real high curb but we hit it pretty good.

So we sent Violet in; and she went in and called a cab and they came and got us and we left. We left the car there. The cops never even knew we were involved in it.

The next morning Bill Siddons picked up Jim's car and had it repaired.

In one of his songs, Jim sings, as if it were a prayer, "Don't let me die in an automobile." When Babe was driving there were no accidents. Why didn't Babe drive more often?

That wasn't the point. You're talking about a death ride. We had death rides. You were on a couple of them.

I don't want to remember.

He took Paul on one. In the alley behind the Whiskey.

I was on that one, in the back seat and Paul was in the front Jim went down the alley behind the Whiskey in the wrong direction, sixty miles an hour.

Yeah, he liked to do that.

Weaving.

No, you can't weave. It's too narrow.

He was weaving.

TESTING

During the filming of HYW Jim said he wanted a panorama of the night lights of Los Angeles. A classmate of ours from the UCLA film school provided access to the roof of the 9000 Building, a highrise on Sunset. Once the equipment and crew were on the roof, Jim surprised everyone by jumping up onto a narrow raised ledge that bordered the top of the building. He informed us that he wanted to be filmed walking along the ledge. No one could talk him out of it. The shot he had in mind would show him walking step by careful step on the edge of the world with the bejeweled Los Angeles night sparkling behind him.

He rejected a rope and ignored our advice that without lights he would appear, at best, a vague shadow blocking the city's lights.

As he began his walk we held our breath fully aware that a missed step could send him hurtling to the hard surface thirty stories below. Why'd he take such a risk?

That's a very hard question to answer. The obvious answer is that he was waiting for someone to jump up and grab him and prove their friendship. I don't think so. I think that among the people that he really liked he felt an inferiority complex.

I saw no particular point in it and I just remember my attitude was if you fall, fuck you. Go on and fall, you're not putting me on no fucking trip about this. Because that's what I thought he was trying to do.

We had been drinking that day and drinking continued as we were filming.

He wasn't quite as drunk as I seen him a lot of times. If he had been,

I would have yanked his ass off there. I would have dove and grabbed his leg. Or just walked over and clipped him. He was just sober enough to have control, like everybody stay away from me and don't touch me. He wasn't that drunk.

Another thing about all these goddamn testing things he did, you never knew just how far along he was. He could be just far enough along that the guy's out of control and you have to take control of him yourself, or he's still got control. You never quite knew. As long as he wasn't running his numbers on me, I'd just sit back and watch him run his numbers on other people, or run his numbers on himself.

NO KIND OF DRUGS

It was just an absolute coincidence that we were on acid when we heard about the deaths of Janis Joplin (*September 18, 1970*) and Jimi Hendrix (*October 4,1970*). I remember taking acid down here at the beach and walking around with these stewardesses. We had great times on it. Happy, hilarious, laughing times.

And Jim never went on any bummer trips when he was on hallucinogenics, not around me. I think it was probably 'cause we were

Bill Siddons, Babe, Jim and Paul Ferrara.

drinking with it. We'd just sit there and toss down half pints. And just get drunk, stoned, laugh.

As you know, he wasn't too much into marijuana. He told me, early on, "It turned on me. I don't enjoy it any more."

We did a lot of cocaine for about eight to ten days, when he and Michael McClure were working on that screenplay about the cocaine dealer, "St. Nicholas." And then after that we'd dabble. Nothing on a regular basis. Heroin, never.

He told me sheepishly that on one trip he took to Europe, that someone gave him a big piece of hashish and he ate it and he forgot about it, and someone else gave him another big piece, and he was drunk and forgot he ate the first piece and he ate the second piece. Well, they had to take him to the hospital and there were nuns there taking care of him and he was so embarrassed, 'cause these nuns knew what he had done. They're in there changing his linen and not allowing him any privacy.

He did take drugs, I seen him do it, we did it. But the man was definitely not into drugs. All the time I knew him, the guy was absolutely into no kind of drugs on a regular basis.

BLOTTO
One of the subjects that Jim would never bring up was his celebrity status. It was as if it shamed him.

There again, you can't know unless you are the one in the eye of the hurricane. It's a two-edged deal. For one thing it gives you an audience for your poetry, while at the same time it takes away your credence as a poet, as a serious poet. I think it was just a phenomenon that he accepted and exploited like he would. With his intellect and his genius, this is a godsend. You get to explore this phenomenon.

I don't think it was a negative thing. Maybe it turned out that way, the way he used it. What he used was the vague grey area between sanity and insanity, which was drunkenness. He'd get as drunk as he could possibly get and go out there and freelance off the top of his head, whatever he was doing, what the people could put up with, how far he could take an audience, anything like that. He certainly didn't plan anything. He didn't plan what he was going to do when he got out on a stage. He didn't plan falling off the stage at the Shrine Auditorium, or he didn't plan all the things he did that got him banned. He just said, I'm going to get as drunk as I can possibly get and then I won't be responsible. It'll just be the phenomenon manifesting itself through me while I'm blotto.

MIAMI
In Miami we knew what was going on. It was a witch hunt. All we had to do is be there and sit there and not make it any worse because we knew what was going to happen at the end.

"I contend an abiding sense of irony over all I do."

(from one of Jim's unpublished notebooks)

We were talking about Jim's bust in Miami and the subsequent trial which had caused tremendous inconvenience and financial loss for the band.

In the end Jim was acquitted of the felony, lewd behavior, and one of the three misdemeanors, public drunkenness. And he was found guilty of profanity and public exposure. Both convictions were immediately appealed. Babe stayed with Jim through the course of the trial and when it was over they traveled back to the West Coast together.

You know that happened all on a Sunday, right. That was another one of those Judge Murry Goodman ploys. They wanted to put Jim in jail so bad. That's why this all came down on a Sunday, so that it would be hard for him to make bail. That's why he set the bail at $50,000 when the fine for what he had just been convicted of was only $500. They were going to put this guy in jail, even if it was overnight, they didn't care.

But Max (*Max Fink, Jim's attorney*) had a check all ready. And we were gone, like the next day, that's it. We were out of there. We drove back. We wanted to see the country, get away.

Tanned and bearded and happy to be on the road, they stopped in Clearwater where Jim showed Babe the place he lived while attending classes at St. Petersburg Junior College. But trouble was still following him and they got thrown in jail for what Babe describes as, "…creating a disturbance or something."

They put us in jail for six or eight hours, something like that. Then they just let us go because they didn't really have any reason to hold us. So from there we went to Tallahassee where Jim went to school (*Florida State*) and saw where he use to live, as a student. We headed straight for New Orleans and got drunk as a couple of walruses.

In Tennessee we hit the speed trap. We go by this car parked in the median, like on the interstate. We don't think anything about it. About a mile up the road there's this guy flagging us over. "Follow me," he says. We get off the highway and we drive about three miles on over into this sleepy little town. There's a judge, "Hundred bucks," he says. We give him the cash. "OK," he says, "you can go."

During all this stuff Jim is totally resigned. To Jim it was a joke, if not a joke it was something to experience, something to laugh about as you drove out of town.

SHRUG IT OFF

In popular rock 'n' roll mythology, Jim was reputed to have been in numerous fights and bar-smashing incidents.

I never seen him do anything violent. Other than maybe drive a car. The guy was not a violent person. I never saw him choose anybody off or anything like that. Or swing at anybody. Or even yell at anybody.

Opposite: On stage in Miami, March 1, 1969. Jim gave a charged performance that was both highly theatrical and controversial.

Oh, he'd yell and call somebody a nigger from time to time, for provocation, not in violence or anger or anything. Violence was totally not part of his personality, of any kind.

I don't think I ever saw him get mad enough to seriously disrupt his disposition.

Fishing in the Caribbean with Babe and Max Fink.

If the guy had anything to get mad about it was about being misquoted or articles about him that weren't true, but even then that wouldn't even begin to incite him to any kind of violence. Or vitriol. He'd just shrug it off, and next time he'd be more careful about what he said so he couldn't be misquoted, or misunderstood in the next interview. As far as what they said without talking to him, he just accepted that as part of the job.

Remember that fight we got into in J. Sloan's that night? Upstairs with the pool table?

I remembered that we were playing pool and two big drunken Chicanos wanted us off the table and Babe didn't quite see it that way, and so there were words and postures and suddenly adrenaline was making every gesture crystal clear.

Jim was great, man. I cracked that pool cue in half and I had a spear and I was going after that big fat guy in the corner and Jim just jumped in the middle and goes, "Babe, the cops, the cops."

As it turns out there were no cops, but Jim's shouting sent our two large adversaries out the door and into the night in a hurry. He might not have been much of a barroom brawler, but he could think quick on his feet.

BACK ON THE TRACK

Pam had little use for most of Jim's friends and would cut us off, most times, with a steely stare. I asked Babe why Pam didn't like us.

Well, you would have to know Pam to know that and we didn't know Pam that well.

Did Jim ever say why she didn't like us?

No, he never made excuses for her, did he. Or try to explain her.

I got along with Pam, when they went to London or somewhere and Pam had that little place in Topanga, I went down there and I took care of Sage (*Jim and Pam's dog*) and the place for a month or two. And we drove down there and we just got along together famously. She thought everybody was taking advantage of Jim and riding on his coattails and we just hit it off, as if me and Jim didn't have that kind of relationship.

That was her whole thing about being against the other Doors, and the office and everything else. It didn't have to do with that they weren't making money, it was just that they were wasting his creativity.

I figure she had a very supportive influence on his poetry and never missed a chance to rag on him when he went off the track. And when he went off fucking around she was always on his ass to get back on the track of his poetry.

Let's face it, none us knew what went on behind that closed door between them two. It was a stormy, love-filled relationship, full of everything: acrimony, making up, the whole deal. When you come right down to it, they loved each other. And he definitely didn't love another woman anywhere near as much. He had a lot of other girl friends and he treated them so gentlemanly that some of them invented things and some of them assumed things, but no, there was no one but Pam, and history bears it out: he was with her from the beginning to the end.

POETRY & PERSONA

As secretive as Jim was about his past, he was even more guarded with his writings, never showing anyone but Pam the contents of his notebooks. And rarely did he read or recite a poem except on stage where his poetic gifts often went unappreciated by audiences waiting and expecting to hear a medley of The Doors' greatest hits.

I think he felt a frustration that he had been born at the wrong time, that poets like himself…it was just the wrong era for it. Like that thing we went to in San Diego (*a symposium of the arts bringing together poets, writers, and filmmakers during the summer of 1969*) with Creeley and Brautigan and all these guys. And he'd look at them and say, "These guys aren't known. I'm better known than these guys and they have more talent than I do. I look up to these people and nobody even knows them."

So it was like an apathy towards life in general because you knew you were not going to be recognized for what you are, who you are deep down inside. Our society does not cater to poets, or recognize them or even know about them.

I just think he was trapped somewhere in a persona he didn't envision for himself and there he was and he had the supreme insight into it. From only his perspective could you understand the real depth and implications of all this. I don't think he really had anything to live for.

What's a guy going to do? His poetry was going to be totally overshadowed for the rest of his life by his name. Whenever poetry circles got together and invited Jim Morrison, they were inviting him, not for his poetry, but for his name.

MADNESS

Sometimes you can be at the center of an event and miss its meaning; or you can share an experience with someone you feel close to and come away with an entirely different reaction. Even though I knew this I wasn't ready for Babe's next set of observations.

Jim was on a path of destruction.

Wait a minute. What do you mean? From the very beginning?

Yeah…We all knew that. Not from the very beginning, but early on.

Babe stared at me.

Why else would he drink like that and get so drunk where he knew that he was going to kill himself. Like those death rides we use to go on in the car. He knew the day after what he had done and he knew that he was going to get that drunk, do it again. And he knew it was either going to end in a fiery James Dean death, or not. Frank, you know this!

Opposite: Onstage in Cleveland, 1968.

Los Angeles, 1970.

I don't know that Jim had a death wish.

Not a wish. Not a wish. That's a cliche that does not apply to this man. Rather say an apathy toward future life. He was exploring drunkenness. Look at it this way: when he got all tied up into that Doors stuff and he became a national hero, that all became ashes, right? And then he had no true goal after that except his poetry, but he could never be taken seriously as a poet. He was always going to be considered as this maverick rock star, that's all they were going to think about it, that he was another crazy rock star. Plus his alienation from his family, deep down inside we were all children, hugging our mothers and sucking their tits. With love and everything. That alienation is not natural.

Did he knew where all this was leading?

Oh, yeah, he was courageous. He had the intelligence to know that madness leads to more madness. And it had no constructive end to it, that he could not come out the other side and say, "I proved something, or I did something." That would be courageous to know that at the end of it was just madness, death, and destruction.

PARIS

If he was so damn bent on self-annihilation why did he go to Paris? Wasn't it to perfect his art and reform his life?

Just a change, get away from everything here.

In the weeks immediately before leaving for Paris Jim seemed to be making positive changes.

He was very sober, he was very sober. He hadn't been hanging around with me that much. We hadn't been getting drunk together. He

Miami, 1970.

seemed like he was trying to divorce himself from everything in a kinda sober, final way. And I was going, "Hey, that's great, man. All the luck."

He was concentrating more and more and more on his poetry and his publishing and that's all he wanted to do was get away from here and get it all behind him.

Towards the end he was starting to take a longer view of things. He knew that whole phenomenon of The Doors was over. He was burnt out, certainly, on concerts, and on records, being in the studio, all that stuff.

He was going to get away but by that time, when that alcohol disease has got ya, you can't get away from it and it's just so easy to go down to the pub and you have a bunch of people around buying you drinks, you love to do it, and you love that feeling of being drunk and the next thing you know you've been doing it for all those years.

Did he recognize that?

I'm sure he did. The guy was too intelligent, I mean knowing about the disease and doing something about it is two different things. You know it's like trying to quit smoking only a lot harder.

HITCHHIKER
I mentioned to Babe that in several of Jim's songs and poems he uses the same two lines:

The hitchiker stood by the side of the road...

And leveled his thumb in the calm calculus of reason

Babe laughed softly.

That's the whole thing of life. I don't know, man. That's just too beautiful to define. You define it within yourself, but to try to describe it, you can't.

He saw himself as the ultimate hitchhiker with no future and no past, and no present, no hope of any of these things. The ultimate existential moment or whatever.